W9-AWG-481

FAMOUS LIVES

The Story of
DAVY CROCKETT
Frontier Hero

FAMOUS LIVES
titles in Large-Print Editions:

FAMOUS LIVES

The Story of
DAVY CROCKETT
Frontier Hero

By Walter Retan
Illustrated By Steven James Petruccio

Gareth Stevens Publishing
MILWAUKEE

For Elizabeth

For a free color catalog describing Gareth Stevens Publishing's list of high-quality books and multimedia programs, call 1-800-542-2595 (USA) or 1-800-461-9120 (Canada). Gareth Stevens Publishing's Fax: (414) 225-0377. See our catalog, too, on the World Wide Web: http://gsinc.com

Library of Congress Cataloging-in-Publication Data

Retan, Walter.
   The story of Davy Crockett: frontier hero / by Walter Retan; illustrated by Steven James Petruccio.
      p. cm. — (Famous lives)
   Includes index.
   Summary: Describes the life of Davy Crockett, one of the Old West's outstanding hunters, frontiersmen, and legislators.
      ISBN 0-8368-1485-1 (lib. bdg.)
      1. Crockett, Davy, 1786-1836—Juvenile literature.   2. Pioneers—Tennessee—Biography—Juvenile literature.   3. Tennessee—Biography—Juvenile literature.   4. Legislators—United States—Biography—Juvenile literature.   5. United States. Congress. House—Biography—Juvenile literature.   [1. Crockett, Davy, 1786-1836.   2. Pioneers.   3. Legislators.]
   I. Petruccio, Steven, ill.   II. Title.   III. Series: Famous lives (Milwaukee, Wis.)
   F436.C95R48   1997
   976.8'04'092—dc21
      [B]   97-3938

The events described in this book are true. They have been carefully researched and excerpted from authentic biographies, writings, and commentaries. No part of this biography has been fictionalized. To learn more about Davy Crockett, refer to the list of books and videos at the back of this book, or ask your librarian to recommend other fine books and videos.

First published in this edition in North America in 1997 by
Gareth Stevens Publishing
1555 North RiverCenter Drive, Suite 201
Milwaukee, Wisconsin 53212 USA

Original © 1993 by Parachute Press, Inc., as a Yearling Biography. Illustrations © 1993 by Steven James Petruccio. Published by arrangement with Bantam Doubleday Dell Books for Young Readers, a division of Bantam Doubleday Dell Publishing Group, Inc. Additional end matter © 1997 by Gareth Stevens, Inc.

Printed in the United States of America

1 2 3 4 5 6 7 8 9 01 00 99 98 97

Contents

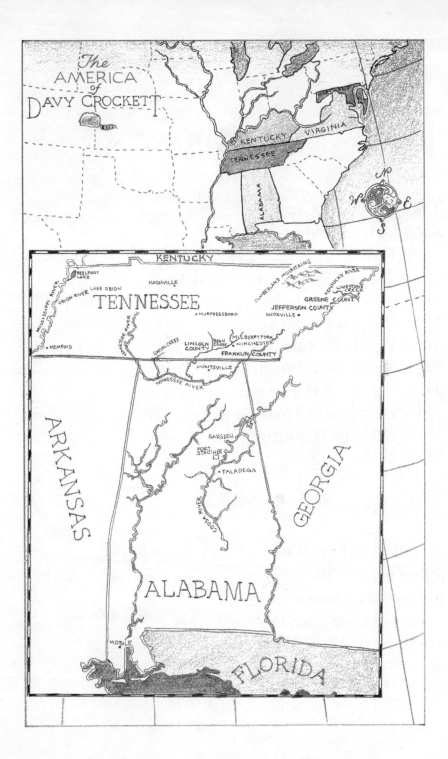

The Two Davy Crocketts

There are two Davy Crocketts. One is the real man—the one who fought in the Creek Indian wars, won fame as a sharpshooter and bear hunter, and was elected to Congress. This Davy Crockett even thought he might someday be president of the United States.

The other Davy Crockett is the man of legend. He is the larger-than-life Davy Crockett that people created in their imaginations. Storytellers had Davy doing just about everything from wrestling bears and steering an alligator up Niagara Falls to straddling a bolt of lightning and catching a flaming comet by the tail.

This book tells the story of the real Davy Crockett. His adventures fighting Creek warriors, hunting bears, and braving the Mississippi River are amazing enough without being exaggerated into "tall tales." But you'll read about some of the tall tales, too. A book about Davy Crockett wouldn't be complete without saying that Davy loved to tell humorous and eye-popping stories. Later, people would make up tales about Davy that were far more outrageous than Davy himself could have imagined.

Davy wrote about some of his adventures in his autobiography, *A Narrative of the Life of David Crockett of the State of Tennessee*. Many of the quotes in this book come from it. Hearing Davy's own words helps to give the full flavor of this colorful frontiersman. As you

1

read the story of the real Davy Crockett, try to spot some of the adventures that storytellers could have later puffed up into enormous tall tales.

Davy's First Adventure

A little boy with an angry red face stood by the side of the river. His name was Davy Crockett. Davy was fighting mad. His four older brothers had paddled out onto the river in a canoe, and they hadn't let Davy go with them. Instead they had taken a neighbor named Campbell. Campbell was about fifteen years old. All of Davy's brothers were younger than that. As for Davy, he couldn't have been more than four or five—and he hated being left out of things just because he was the youngest.

The Crockett brothers were used to paddling the canoe. They could have guided it safely anywhere on the river. But Campbell wouldn't let them. He thought he should hold the paddle because he was older. The only problem was that Campbell had never steered a canoe before.

A short way down the river there was a steep waterfall. The canoe began to drift dangerously close to it. Although Campbell paddled furiously, he couldn't control the canoe. It was headed straight toward the falls.

Little Davy stood on the shore, watching. He could see what was happening to his brothers, but he was so angry at them that he didn't care. For the moment, anyway, he felt it would serve them right if the canoe went crashing over the falls.

Fortunately a farmer named Kendall was working in a field nearby. He saw that the boys were in danger.

Quickly he ran toward the river, throwing off his coat and shirt at the same time. By the time he plunged into the cold water, he was wearing nothing but his short pants.

The sight of Kendall crashing through the water frightened Davy. He began to scream wildly, but Kendall paid no attention. The farmer was chasing after the canoe as fast as he could go. Where the water was deep, he swam. Where it was shallow, he slid his feet over the slippery stones. Finally he caught up with the canoe when it was only a few feet from the waterfall. The current was so swift there that the force of the water almost pulled the canoe right over the falls. But Kendall held on to the canoe with all his might. By some miracle he managed to stop the canoe and pull it out of danger.

When the boys got back to shore, Davy realized that they were more frightened than he. Davy later said, "The only thing that comforted me was the belief that it was a punishment on them for leaving me on shore."

It's interesting that this is the only story from his early childhood that Davy later chose to write about in his autobiography. The story shows perfectly the kind of stubbornness, strong will, and independence that would be such an important part of Davy all his life. He never put up with bad treatment or insults, and he always hated to be left out of anything—especially anything exciting or adventurous.

The canoe experience took place in what is now eastern Tennessee, near where Limestone Creek enters the Nolachucky River. Here Davy Crockett was

born on August 17, 1786, in a rough little log cabin built by nis father, John Crockett.

The American Revolution had ended only three years earlier. John Crockett had fought bravely against the British. He had also served as a frontier ranger in his county militia. Three years before Davy's birth, his grandfather—also named David—and his grandmother had been killed in an Indian raid on their small farm in eastern Tennessee.

Like most frontiersmen of his day, John Crockett was a poor man, but he had had a little education. He served in the local government and was able to sign his own name to bills of sale and court orders. Many frontiersmen of the time couldn't write their own names.

The Crockett family moved several times during Davy's early childhood. His father would buy one or two hundred acres of land, hoping he could later sell it at a higher price to settlers traveling westward in search of land. After selling one piece of land, he would move farther west and buy another. This was a common practice among frontier farmers. They tried to pay off their debts by buying land, improving it, and then selling it at a profit.

In 1794, when Davy was about eight years old, the family moved to Cove Creek in Greene County, Tennessee. John Crockett built a flour mill there. Unfortunately, a flood destroyed the mill before it had a chance to do much business. Davy later wrote, "I remember the water rose so high that it got up into the house we lived in, and my father moved us out of it to keep us from being drowned."

6

After the mill disaster, the family moved to Jefferson County. Here John Crockett bought a small tavern on the road between Knoxville, Tennessee, and Abingdon, Virginia. Taverns were places that offered food as well as lodging to travelers. John Crockett's tavern was a very simple log building with a few small rooms. The tavern mainly served hunters and wagoners who traveled the road with supplies. Davy was supposed to help with the chores—carrying pails of water, feeding the travelers' horses, and tending crops that grew in the surrounding fields. But he didn't much like the work. What he did enjoy was listening to the tales that travelers told at night by the fireplace.

They described strange, mysterious caves in the mountains to the west. They also told fantastic tales about huge snapping turtles with shells as big as barrels and heads as big as a boy's head. Hunters bragged about feats of amazing marksmanship. They told of sharpshooters so skillful that their bullets could cut the string off a soaring kite or shoot a high-flying goose out of the sky. And they told scary stories, too, about being attacked by giant black bears and savage, roving Indians. Some of what the travelers said was probably true. Some was not. Telling such exaggerated stories was popular at the time, and that is probably where Davy first learned about tall tales. He was to become famous for telling such stories himself.

One day an old German farmer named Jacob Siler stopped at the tavern. He had come to Tennessee to buy cattle, and he was driving a large herd back to his Virginia farm. He must have been impressed by young Davy, because he asked Mr. Crockett if he could hire the boy to help him manage the herd. The pair would have to travel about four hundred miles on foot. Siler agreed to pay Davy six dollars for his services.

Davy's father was so poor that he agreed to let his twelve-year-old son go off with the complete stranger. Children in those days often had to earn their own keep. By now there were nine Crockett children and almost no money to feed and clothe them.

Davy later wrote that at first Jacob Siler was very kind to him. Some historians even think that the old man may have taught Davy how to use one of the new, superior German rifles. But when they reached the Siler farm, the old man wanted Davy to remain there and not go back to his family. Because Davy had been taught to obey his elders, he felt he had no choice but to stay. Although he tried to act contented as he worked around the farm, he was very unhappy.

One Sunday afternoon Davy was playing alongside the road with two neighbor boys. Suddenly three wagons came along. They were driven by an old man named Dunn and his two sons. The three men were on their way to Knoxville, carrying goods for trading. In those days settlers on the frontier depended on wagoners to bring their supplies of flour, sugar, molasses, and other things. They returned to the east-coast cities with corn, rye, and other farm produce.

Wagoners were a rough bunch, but they were also good-hearted and friendly. Davy recognized the Dunns because they had often stopped at his father's tavern as they traveled their routes. Davy told the men how unhappy he was and asked if they would help him get back to his family.

Mr. Dunn said that he and his sons planned to spend the night at a nearby tavern. If Davy could get to them before daylight the next morning, the wagoners would take him home. Mr. Dunn even promised to protect Davy if Jacob Siler tried to catch up with him.

Davy rushed back to the Siler farmhouse. Luckily no one was around. The family had gone to visit a neighbor. Davy gathered up his clothes and money and hid them under his bed. He went to bed early, but couldn't fall asleep. He was too excited by the idea of seeing his family again. He was also worried that he might be discovered escaping from the house the next morning.

About three hours before dawn, Davy quietly slipped out of the house with his little bundle. He discovered that a heavy snow was falling. It was already nearly eight inches deep. Davy had a difficult time finding the road because the falling snow blotted out the moonlight. He had to guide himself by the opening the road made between the trees. Soon the snow was practically to his knees, but he kept pushing ahead. At least Jacob Siler wouldn't be able to follow Davy's tracks. The snow was covering everything.

By the time Davy reached the tavern, the wagoners were already up and about. They were feeding their horses and getting their equipment ready for the trip. Mr. Dunn welcomed the boy, treating him with great kindness. He told Davy to warm himself by the fire. Then the little group ate an early breakfast and set off on their journey. To Davy the trip seemed to take forever. By now his thoughts were so much on his family that he couldn't wait to get home.

At last the wagoners reached Roanoke, Virginia, where Davy decided to go ahead on foot. He felt he could travel twice as fast as the wagons. Mr. Dunn tried to talk him out of leaving the wagon party, but Davy had his heart set on getting home just as quickly as possible. He stayed overnight in Roanoke, then started off early the next morning.

After Davy had been walking for some time, a gentleman rode up on horseback. He was bringing some horses home from the market. The man had an extra horse fitted out with a bridle and saddle. He invited the boy to ride along beside him. Davy was so tired that he welcomed the chance to ride. He was lucky because he was close to the Roanoke River, and without the horse he would have been forced to wade through the freezing-cold water.

Davy rode beside the kind stranger until they were within fifteen miles of John Crockett's house. There they parted. Davy set off for home.

That night there was a joyous reunion in the Crockett household, and Davy was the center of attention as he told his family about his many adventures.

Davy Runs Away

The following fall John Crockett decided that Davy should go to school with his older brothers. Davy was now thirteen years old and couldn't yet read or write. For four days Davy attended a small country school run by a man named Benjamin Kitchen. Davy had just begun to learn the letters of the alphabet when he got into a quarrel with a much bigger and older student.

Davy was smart enough to know that he shouldn't start a fight while the schoolmaster was around. Instead he waited until late afternoon, when the older pupils would be finishing up their lessons. Then he slipped out of the schoolhouse and walked some distance down the road. Hiding behind a clump of thick bushes, he waited for the bully to come along. When the larger boy came walking down the road, Davy jumped out from behind the bushes, taking him by surprise.

"I set on him like a wildcat," Davy said. "I scratched his face all to a flitter jig and soon made him cry out for quarter (mercy)."

When Davy got home that day, he said nothing to his parents about the fight, and he asked his brothers not to tell on him. The next morning he started out for school as usual. But instead of going to the schoolhouse with his brothers, Davy hid all day in the woods. He knew that if he went to school, Mr. Kitchen would whip him with a hickory stick. That might hurt worse

11

than the beating Davy had given his enemy.

In the late afternoon, when his brothers started home from their classes, Davy joined them on the road. For several days he continued to hide out during school hours. He enjoyed roaming through the wild woods. He studied deep buffalo paths left by herds that had once lived there. He watched deer gliding silently through thick bushes and spied on wildcats crouching in tall sycamore trees. Davy liked the woodlands far more than he liked Mr. Kitchen's classroom.

One morning a note arrived for John Crockett. It was from Mr. Kitchen. The schoolmaster asked why Davy had not been sent to school for several days. As soon as Davy's father read the note, he shouted for his son to come talk to him. He wanted to know why the boy hadn't been at school. Davy replied that he didn't dare go because he was afraid the schoolmaster would whip him. His father said that *he* would whip him a good deal worse if Davy didn't go back to school immediately. Davy foolishly tried to argue, and his father lost his temper. Grabbing a thick stick, Mr. Crockett started after his son.

Now Davy knew he was in real trouble! He started to run down the road as fast as he could—*away* from the schoolhouse. Mr. Crockett followed hot on his heels. They had gone almost a mile when Davy spied a hill. He headed for it. As soon as he had passed over the peak, he turned to one side and hid behind some bushes. Soon his father tore past, never seeing Davy. Finally Mr. Crockett gave up and returned home. Davy came out of his hiding place and headed for a

neighbor's farm a few miles away.

The farmer's name was Jesse Cheek, and he was about to start for Front Royal, Virginia, with a herd of cattle. Davy hired himself out to go along. He decided that both his home and the schoolhouse were too dangerous for him. One of his older brothers had already been hired to go on the drive, so Davy would be in good company on the trip.

As soon as the group reached Front Royal, Davy decided to start home immediately with Jesse Cheek's brother. Leaving the group behind probably wasn't the best idea, but the strong-willed Davy had made up his mind. He didn't want to wait for the rest of the party—and once Davy made up his mind about something there was no stopping him. Unfortunately Davy and his companion had just one horse between them, and the older man never wanted to stop to rest. Davy decided to continue on his own. The man gave him just four dollars for spending money.

Davy bought some food supplies, then started off by himself. Before long he met a wagoner from Greeneville, Tennessee, who was taking a load to Gerardstown, Virginia. The wagoner's name was Adam Myers. He seemed a friendly, good-natured man, and he invited Davy to make the trip with him. He promised that they would return to Tennessee as soon as he had made the delivery in Virginia.

When they arrived at Gerardstown, the wagoner couldn't find a load to take back to Tennessee. He had to settle for some local hauling jobs. While Davy waited for Mr. Myers, he went to work for a farmer named John Gray. He was paid only twenty-five cents a day, but the work wasn't hard. By spring he had enough money to buy some new clothes. He decided to go with Mr. Myers on the wagoner's next trip to Baltimore, Maryland. Davy had never been to a city, and he wanted to see what kind of place a city was. He still had almost seven dollars left from his wages. These he gave to Mr. Myers for safekeeping.

In Baltimore they had to wait for some repairs on the wagon, so Davy decided to go down to the docks. He was amazed to see the big ships with their huge white sails flapping in the breeze. Filled with curiosity, Davy finally worked up enough nerve to step aboard one of the ships. He was met on the deck by the captain, who asked if Davy wouldn't like to sail to London on the ship. The idea of a trip fascinated Davy. By now he was used to being away from home and was eager for adventure. He agreed to sign on for the trip, explaining to the captain that he would go get his clothes and return right away.

When Davy told Adam Myers that he had come for his money and clothes because he was sailing to London, the wagoner refused to give them to him. In fact, he threatened to lock the boy in a room and keep him there until it was time for the trip back to Tennessee. Davy was bitterly disappointed, but there was nothing he could do. Myers kept such a close watch on Davy that he had no chance to escape. After a few days, they set off in the wagon.

This time the trip was very unpleasant. Myers treated Davy very badly. Several times he even threatened the boy with his horsewhip. Davy decided that he had to get away. Early one morning he sneaked

15

out of the wagon with just his clothes and took off on foot. He had to leave his money behind.

He had gone several miles when he met another wagoner. Defenseless and penniless, Davy knew that he had to find a friend to help him. When the man asked the boy in a kindly voice where he was going, Davy could not hold back his tears. He explained what had happened to him, including the fact that the other wagoner had kept all his money so that he couldn't even buy some food.

By odd coincidence this new wagoner's name was also Myers—Henry Myers. When he heard Davy's sad story, he was furious, and he promised that he would make the villain give back Davy's money. The wagoner turned his cart around, and they went about two miles before they found Adam Myers. Unfortunately Myers no longer had Davy's money. He didn't even have any of his own money left. He had spent it all in Baltimore.

The boy and his new protector had to be satisfied with Adam Myers's story. They didn't really have any choice. Heading once again toward Tennessee, they continued traveling together until they reached the place where they had to go in different directions. On their last night together they stayed at a tavern where several other wagoners had stopped. Henry Myers explained to the men how badly Davy had been treated. The wagoners were so concerned that they took up a collection. They gave Davy three dollars to help him on his journey.

The money lasted until Davy reached Montgomery, Virginia. He had to stay in the town for more than a year and a half doing odd jobs for people. Finally he earned enough money to buy a few clothes, with some left over to buy food on the trip home.

This time he traveled alone, and everything went well—until he reached New River, Virginia. The waves on the river there were so rough and choppy that nobody dared to take Davy across in a boat. They were afraid they might drown. But Davy refused to be put off. He finally persuaded someone to let him take a canoe and try to get across the river on his own. He tied his bundle of clothes to the canoe so that they wouldn't get away. Then he shoved off into the waves.

It was a wild journey. The gale blew the canoe almost two miles upriver before Davy finally reached the other shore. He felt like a drowned rat in a boat half filled with icy-cold water. Davy's clothes had frozen stiff. But he was so happy to have crossed safely that he scarcely minded.

Davy had to walk three miles before he found a house where he could warm himself and get some hot food and drink.

But Davy didn't want to waste any time. The very next day he started off again. After many days of walking, he finally arrived at the home of his father's brother Joseph. It was wonderful to be back in Tennessee. To Davy's amazement, his older brother—the one who had gone on the cattle drive with him—was also visiting their uncle.

After spending a few weeks with Joseph Crockett, Davy started homeward again. He arrived at his father's tavern at nightfall in the early spring of 1802. He was now almost sixteen years old. He had been away from home for two and a half years. During those years he had grown from a boy to a young man. There was even the beginning of a beard on his face.

Davy decided to see if his family would recognize him now that he looked so much older. Without saying who he was, he asked for a bed for the night. He spoke little and stayed in a dark corner by the fireplace until it was time for supper.

When the guests were called to eat, Davy left his corner and sat down at the table with the wagoners staying at the tavern. So far nobody had recognized him. But his oldest sister began to give him long looks. Suddenly she got up, ran around the table, and seized him around the neck. "Here is my lost brother!" she cried.

When Davy saw how joyful his family was to see him again, he said it "made me sorry that I hadn't submitted to a hundred whippings sooner than cause so much affliction as they had suffered on my account." Overcome by happiness, Mr. Crockett completely forgave Davy for his past mischief.

Davy Takes a Wife

Davy's father still had financial problems. He owed a man named Abraham Wilson thirty-six dollars. Mr. Crockett asked Davy to work six months for Wilson to pay off the debt. Davy agreed. He later wrote, "I . . . worked with all my might, not losing a single day in the six months." But Davy didn't like his employer, and he left just as soon as he had worked off the debt. Davy's father was very pleased by his son's efforts. John Crockett was an honest man who tried hard to get his debts paid.

Unfortunately, he also owed forty dollars to an old Quaker farmer named John Kennedy. Once again Davy came to the rescue. He secretly agreed to work for Kennedy for two shillings a day to pay off his father's debt. Davy worked hard for another six months, not even taking time off to visit his family, though they lived only fifteen miles away. At the end of the six months, Davy proudly returned home and told his father that his debt to Kennedy was now canceled.

Davy enjoyed working for John Kennedy, so he kept working at his farm. He was eager to earn enough money to buy some new clothes.

After about two months had passed, Mr. Kennedy's niece came to visit from North Carolina. For the first time Davy fell in love. He thought she was the most beautiful young woman he had ever seen. He wanted so much to get to know her, but he was too shy to start a conversation. He had no idea what he should say.

Finally he decided that he simply had to say something to her. After several rather shaky attempts, he summoned the courage to tell her how much he admired her. He said that he just had to have her as his wife or he would die.

The young woman appreciated his flattering words, but she explained that she couldn't marry Davy because she was already engaged to marry her cousin, Mr. Kennedy's son.

Davy was crushed, but it was clear to him that his cause was hopeless. He began to think that perhaps his problems all came from his lack of education. He decided to go back to school.

As it happened, Mr. Kennedy had a son who was a schoolmaster and ran a school nearby. Davy arranged to go there for lessons four days a week. As payment, he worked two days for the schoolmaster. This time Davy attended school faithfully, learning to read, write his own name, and do a little work with numbers. He would have stayed in school longer, but now he was more determined than ever to find a wife. Having recovered from his first romantic disappointment, he decided to look for somebody else.

A family named Elder with several very pretty daughters lived in the area. Davy liked the one named Margaret and asked her if he could call on her. Margaret seemed to like Davy, though she had been seeing another young man in the neighborhood. She and Davy began to see each other regularly. Soon Davy was as much in love with Margaret Elder as he had been with Mr. Kennedy's niece. Margaret and Davy decided to get married, and Davy applied for a marriage license at the courthouse.

While the courtship was going on, Davy was also developing another interest. He had been perfecting his skill with a long rifle. Frequently he slipped off into the woods to shoot a deer or some other kind of game. He began to carry his rifle wherever he went. Often he took part in rifle-shooting contests. He handled his hunting tools like an experienced marksman. First he would blow through the rifle barrel to make sure it was clear. Then, with a turn of his wrist, he'd put in a bullet and fill the powder pan. His skillful lift of the gun, his swift, easy aim, and the drop of the rifle all seemed to be accomplished in one single curving movement. He had already won many small prizes, but he wanted something better.

About a week before his marriage, Davy went off to another shooting contest. This time the prize was a whole beef. Davy won it easily. He sold his prize for five gold dollars, then joined in the country dancing and merrymaking that followed the contest. Word of his behavior reached his fiancée. She thought he should be spending his time with her.

A day or two later he went to visit Margaret. On the way he stopped at her uncle's house. Margaret's younger sister was there. She looked so serious and embarrassed that Davy realized something must be wrong. As soon as he had a chance to talk to her alone, he asked what was troubling her. She immediately burst into tears. Her sister, she said, was going to marry another man the next day. Davy's behavior had

21

made her angry.

Davy was stunned. How could his beloved be so disloyal? The younger sister urged him to go to Margaret and try to change her mind. She assured him that both she and her parents preferred Davy to the other man.

Davy, however, was so bitter about Margaret's unfaithfulness that he refused to see her again. He decided that he "was only born for hardships, misery, and disappointment." For a long time he moped about and showed little interest in things. But Davy could nurse his sorrow just so long. In a few months he was out looking for a wife again.

Once more he began to attend dances. When there was work like planting and harvesting to be done, young men and women would come from miles around to help. Once the job was finished, they got together for a "frolic," as the dances were called.

Davy didn't tell his Quaker employer that he went to these dances. Mr. Kennedy wouldn't have approved. Nor did Davy want the old man to know about his shooting contests. The Quakers were peaceful people who didn't believe in the use of firearms except for hunting only the amount of game absolutely required for food.

Another young lad worked on the Kennedy farm, too. He enjoyed dancing as much as Davy did, but the old farmer wouldn't allow him to go to the frolics. One Sunday, while the Kennedy family was at the Quaker meeting, the two boys rigged a tall pole from the ground to their upstairs attic window. On nights when there were dances, they would wait until the

family was asleep, then slide down the pole in their best clothes.

At one of these dances Davy met a beautiful young Irish girl named Mary Finley. Her family called her Polly. Davy and Polly liked each other right away, but Davy soon discovered that he had a rival. Worse yet, Polly's mother favored the rival. This time Davy did not intend to lose out. For several months he had been saving money to buy a horse from his employer. As soon as he had purchased it, he rode to Polly's house in style and asked her to marry him. She agreed immediately. After he left, Davy went directly to his father's house to arrange for the wedding reception. A few days later he returned to Polly's house to ask her parents for permission to marry her.

Polly's mother was furious and refused to hear of a wedding. Polly's father seemed less opposed. Finally Davy told Mrs. Finley that he was going to marry her daughter whether she liked it or not. He told Polly he would be back to get her on the following Thursday. He would bring an extra horse for her to ride, and she should be packed and ready to leave with him.

The following Thursday he rode to his future wife's home with a group of relatives and friends. They arrived at the Finleys' cabin only to find that Polly's mother opposed the marriage as much as ever. But this time Davy wasn't going to wait. He didn't want to lose another prospective wife. When Polly came out with all her belongings, he helped her onto the horse. Then they headed toward the gate.

Polly's father stood at the gate, waiting for them. He apologized for his wife's behavior and asked if

Davy wouldn't stay and be married there. Davy said he was willing if Mrs. Finley would apologize to him. Mr. Finley went into the house, and after a long time he came out with his wife. She apologized to Davy and asked him to stay. She explained that she had never had a child married before, and it was hard for her to face the idea of losing Polly.

Davy sent for the parson, and the couple were married that very day—August 16, 1806—in front of a large group of family members and friends. The next day—Davy's twentieth birthday—everybody went to John Crockett's tavern for a big wedding celebration.

When Polly and Davy returned to the Finley home, Polly's mother was in very good spirits. She gave them two fine cows and two calves. Davy later wrote: "Though it was a small marriage portion, it was much better than I expected."

Davy rented a small farm with a cabin, and there he went with his new wife. He wondered how they could ever afford to buy anything to put in the cabin. To his great surprise, John Kennedy arranged for Davy to get credit at a neighboring store for fifteen dollars' worth of items that Polly might choose.

Davy and Polly worked on the farm for several years. Their two sons—John Wesley and William— were born there. But the couple just couldn't seem to make much money. Davy decided that they should move before the family got any bigger. He wanted to go farther west in Tennessee, to Elk River country. That frontier was just beginning to attract settlers. Polly's father offered to go along, taking an extra horse to help carry their belongings. Davy and Polly had one old horse and two young colts. They loaded as many of their possessions as they could onto the two colts and the extra horse, and in the fall of 1811 they started on their long journey across the Cumberland Mountains.

Arriving safely in Lincoln County, they settled on the Mulberry fork of the Elk River. It was very rich country, and there was plenty of game. "It was here," Davy later wrote, "that I began to distinguish myself as a hunter . . . of deer and smaller game I killed abundance; but the bear had been much hunted in those parts before, and were not so plenty as I could have wished."

Davy and Polly lived there about two years. Then, early in 1813, they moved to Franklin County, where they settled on Bean's Creek. Their new home was just a few miles north of the present-day Alabama border. Davy called his new homestead Kentuck.

Davy in the Creek War

Davy Crockett and his family weren't the only settlers moving westward. As the east-coast towns and farmlands became crowded, more and more settlers moved into central Tennessee. There they settled on land that the government had set aside for Indians, the settlers' name for the Native American tribes. Conflicts soon began to arise between the settlers and the Indians. The Indians didn't share the European people's tradition of private land ownership. They believed that the land, the forests, and the wild animals existed for the benefit of all people. Sometimes tribes did fight with each other over the use of a certain territory—but never for ownership of it.

The Creek tribes lived in Alabama and in parts of Florida, Georgia, and Tennessee. It was a land full of small creeks running into larger rivers. This is why early white settlers called the region the creek country and called the Native Americans who lived there Creeks.

By the time the white settlers arrived, the Creeks were living very much like them. They built permanent houses and wore clothing made from woven cloth instead of animal skins. Each town had a ruler selected from a leading family. There were laws to cover hunting, marriage, and the conduct of public business. Many of the early settlers intermarried with the Creeks and lived a happy, peaceful life inside the Creek nation.

When Davy and his family moved to Bean's Creek, this state of peace was just coming to an end. A famous northern Shawnee Indian chief, Tecumseh, had decided that there was only one way to stop the steady westward movement of the white settlers who were taking over tribal lands. He believed that the native tribes—from north to south—must unite to drive the white people back to the seacoast.

In October 1812, Tecumseh traveled south to try to get the support of the Creek nation. This trip took place just a few months before Davy and his family moved to Bean's Creek. The Creeks listened to the Shawnee chief with great excitement. He told them that the white settlers would never be satisfied until they had taken over the whole country. Tecumseh urged the Creeks not to adapt to the ways of the settlers. Instead they should be faithful to their own beliefs and traditions.

The chief also explained that the Indian warriors would have the help of the British army. In June the Americans had declared war again on the British (the War of 1812). So far there had been little fighting. But Tecumseh told the Creeks that the British had agreed to supply arms and ammunition for use against the settlers.

The Lower Creeks, who lived in the southern part of present-day Alabama, didn't want a war with the white settlers. But the Upper Creeks, who lived farther north, agreed to support Tecumseh. These were the Creeks who lived closest to the Crockett family on

28

Bean's Creek. Early in 1813 the British landed a small number of men at Pensacola, Florida, and set up a base. They began distributing guns to all Creek warriors who were unfriendly to the Americans.

Three chiefs who had been making raids on white settlements decided to go south to Pensacola to pick up guns and powder. A group of 180 militiamen heard about the expedition and decided to attack the Creeks on their return trip. They took the warriors by surprise, while they were eating. The Creeks fled. But instead of chasing after them, the militiamen began collecting their stores of weapons and ammunition. Meanwhile, one of the chiefs rallied his warriors. They made a surprise counterattack on the unsuspecting Americans, and the soldiers fled in total confusion.

As soon as news of the attack spread, white settlers began to move into forts, seeking protection from such raids. They feared the Creeks might make more attacks. Many settlers gathered around the residence of Samuel Mimms, near the Alabama and Tombigbee rivers. Here they built a square-shaped stockade enclosing almost an acre of land, as well as several buildings. They called it Fort Mimms.

By late August about 550 people had come to the fort. At least 265 were soldiers under the command of Major Daniel Beasley of the Mississippi Volunteers. For some reason Major Beasley didn't seem to take the threat of a Creek attack seriously. He didn't drill his men, and he didn't post any lookouts. He didn't even bother to keep the gates to the fort closed. His men loafed around the stockade playing card games and dancing with the young women who were living in the fort.

At high noon on August 30 the Creeks suddenly attacked the fort. They found the gates wide open and the posts completely undefended. A force of one thousand warriors swarmed through the gate, killing everyone they saw. Then they surrounded the fort and shot flaming arrows at the buildings. The settlers fled from one burning building to another. Those who weren't shot were burned to death. Only seventeen people survived.

News of the massacre at Fort Mimms spread fast. At Nashville the citizens held a mass meeting. They demanded that an expedition be sent against the Creeks. The state legislature voted to call up 2,500 volunteers. The troops would be commanded by General Andrew Jackson. Jackson was a Nashville lawyer who had fought in the American Revolution when he was just fourteen years old.

The news of the attack quickly reached the settlers at Bean's Creek, too. Until now Davy had never met any unfriendly native people. As he later wrote, "There had been no war among us for so long that but few, who were not too old to bear arms, knew anything about the business." Still, when Davy learned that there was to be a general meeting of the local militia in nearby Winchester, he immediately decided that he would join the fighting forces. His wife pleaded with him to remain with her and the children. But Davy believed that enlisting was a duty he owed to his country. He later said, "The truth is, my dander was up, and nothing but war could bring it right again."

Davy and the other men elected a lawyer named Francis Jones as their captain and volunteered for a term of ninety days. Everybody believed the fighting would be over by then. Davy went home to collect his equipment and say good-bye to his wife and sons. He returned to Winchester on horseback, joining the rest of the company. As soon as everyone had assembled, they headed for Beaty's Spring, a little south of Huntsville, Alabama. Here they waited for other troops to join them. In a few days at least 1,300 volunteers had gathered.

While they were waiting for General Jackson to arrive from Nashville so they could join his troops, a Major John Gibson decided to take some militiamen across the Tennessee River to spy on the Creeks. He asked Captain Jones to pick two men who were expert shots. Jones chose Davy and told him to pick the second man. Davy picked a young man named George Russell, but Major Gibson objected. He said that Russell didn't have enough of a beard. Gibson wanted men, not boys. Davy told Gibson that if he measured courage by the length of a beard, he might better choose a goat! The major offered no more arguments.

Early the next morning, thirteen men mounted their horses and set off across the Tennessee River at a place called Ditto's Landing. They separated into two parties and followed two separate roads. The major took seven men, and Davy took four. They

31

planned to meet that evening at the spot where the two roads joined again.

Davy followed his assigned route but wasn't able to learn anything useful about the movements of the Creek warriors. When he arrived at the meeting place, there was no sign of Major Gibson's scouting party. Davy and his men slept overnight in a little hidden hollow off the road. The next morning Gibson's group had still not appeared, so Davy decided to go on without them.

The scouting party continued for more than twenty miles until they came to the house of a white settler named Radcliffe. Radcliffe was married to a Creek woman and lived just at the edge of the Creek nation. The men ate their dinner at his farm and fed their horses. Radcliffe seemed frightened. He told them that ten painted Creek warriors had stopped at his house only an hour earlier. If they came back and found Davy and his soldiers, they would kill Radcliffe and his whole family.

After finishing their dinner, the men saddled their horses. Davy had decided that they should keep going. He was more afraid to return to his company than to go forward. He was sure he would never hear the last of it if he arrived back at camp without any information about the warring Creeks.

The scouting party rode through the Indians' territory by the light of a full moon. Before they had gone far, they met two black slaves who had been seized by the Creeks. The two men, brothers, had escaped with some of the Creeks' ponies and rifles. Both of the men were able to speak the Creeks' language. Davy sent one of the brothers back to Ditto's Landing and asked the other to go with his group.

Late that night the scouting party arrived at the camp of about forty friendly Creek Indians. Davy decided to stay there overnight. The men tied up their horses with their saddles on them, ready to flee if they were attacked. They slept on the ground with their rifles in their arms. Davy had just gotten to sleep when he heard a frightful scream. It was a war scream from a Creek messenger who had just arrived at the camp. He reported that he had seen a huge war party of Creeks crossing the Coosa River at the Ten Islands. They were advancing to meet General Jackson's army.

Davy decided that the time had come to return to his home base. The men mounted their horses and started on the sixty-five-mile trip back to Beaty's Spring. They reached the camp about ten o'clock the next morning. Davy immediately made his report to Colonel John Coffee, who was in temporary command of all the troops at Beaty's Spring. Davy was furious when the colonel didn't pay any attention to him. Not until the following day—when Major Gibson finally returned with the same report—did the colonel react. He immediately sent a runner with a message to General Jackson. Davy realized that the colonel had ignored his report because he was not an officer. Coffee refused to believe the news until he heard it from Major Gibson. This experience made a big impression on Davy. For the rest of his life he resented army "brass," as he called all officers.

As soon as General Jackson received Colonel Coffee's message, he ordered his men to march southward to Beaty's Spring. The troops had to march all night long without any rest. They arrived at the camp the very next day, their feet covered with blisters. After the men had rested, Jackson pushed on into Alabama with his combined forces. As General Jackson and his army marched southward, he ordered the men to build a string of forts to protect their rear. At Coosa River and the Ten Islands (the site of present-day Gadsden, Alabama), they built Fort Strother. Then Jackson sent out spies to look for enemy forces. Word came back that there were unfriendly Creeks in Tallussahatchee, a town about eight miles away. An attack group that included Davy was sent out to destroy the town.

At sunrise on November 3, 1813, the troops secretly surrounded the village. Then they attacked without warning. The warriors tried to fight back, but they were outnumbered. Altogether, 168 Creeks were killed. Only five white soldiers died in the battle. It had been a complete massacre—like the one at Fort Mimms. But this time the Creeks were the victims. When the fighting ended, the troops returned to Fort Strother.

On the night of November 7 a friendly Creek came to the fort, shouting that he had news for General Jackson. He reported that Fort Taladega was surrounded by unfriendly Creek warriors. They had threatened to seize the fort and ammunition if the Creeks living inside didn't come out to help fight the white soldiers.

When Jackson's troops drew near Fort Taladega,

the general divided his forces so that they would pass to both the right and left of the fort. Then they were to close the gaps at the front and rear, forming a tight square around the area. By doing this, the general planned to trap the enemy Creeks camped around the fort.

But the Creeks had their own plan. Nearly a thousand warriors—painted scarlet red—had hidden behind the bank of a stream that circled the far end of the fort, making a kind of half-moon shape. Jackson's men couldn't see them, so they continued to advance straight ahead. Suddenly the Creek warriors leaped from their hiding place, screaming war whoops and shooting their guns. The militiamen fired back, but in the excitement they broke ranks. In spite of the heavy fire, nearly seven hundred of the Creek warriors escaped. Three hundred were killed. Jackson's forces lost only seventeen men.

By this time the weather was turning cold in Alabama. The volunteers' clothes were nearly worn out, and their horses had grown weak and thin. Many of the men had served their ninety days and were ready to go home. Davy was one of them. He had been in enough fighting to last him awhile. And the brutal treatment of the Creeks had begun to appall him. On December 8, 1813, he was officially discharged from the army and returned to Tennessee.

For about eight months Davy stayed at home, working on the farm with Polly and the children. During that time General Jackson and his troops defeated a large Creek force in a great victory at the battle of Horseshoe Bend. Six months later, on August 10,

1814, Jackson signed a treaty with the Creeks, ending the hostilities.

But the war against the British continued, so on September 28, 1814, Davy volunteered again. He wanted to see what it would be like to fight British soldiers. This time he joined the militia with the rank of 3rd sergeant. Unfortunately, instead of fighting the British, Davy's company was assigned to look for enemy Creeks hiding in the wilderness of Alabama. He served out his six-month enlistment period and then returned home. There was no longer any possibility of fighting British soldiers. The War of 1812 was over, and the United States had defeated Great Britain.

Davy Runs for Office

By March 1815, Davy was back home. Now twenty-eight years old, he had left the militia with the rank of 4th sergeant. His honesty and capable leadership must have impressed his men. In May he was elected lieutenant in the 32nd Regiment of the Tennessee militia.

A new baby was waiting for Davy at the Crockett home. Polly had given birth to their third child, a little girl she had named Margaret. The family was happy to be together again, and Davy enjoyed getting back to work on his farm. But his happiness didn't last long. In midsummer Polly grew sick and died. There is no record of the cause of her illness or even of the exact date when she died.

Polly's death was a great blow to Davy. He later wrote that she had been an "affectionate good mother . . . and a tender and loving wife." Now he was all alone with three children, the youngest still an infant. He asked his youngest brother, who was married, to bring his family and live on Davy's farm. His brother and sister-in-law tried hard to look after Davy and the children, but life for Davy just wasn't the same as it had been with Polly. Finally Davy decided that he should marry again.

There happened to be a widow in the neighborhood whose husband had been killed in the Creek war. Her name was Elizabeth Patton. She had a small boy and girl of her own. Davy admired her and

ST. JAMES SCHOOL LIBRARY
HIGHWOOD, ILLINOIS

thought they might get along well. He began to pay regular visits to her and discovered that she seemed to like him. When he asked her to marry him, she accepted.

Elizabeth Patton came from a prominent family in North Carolina. Her father was quite well-to-do, and Elizabeth herself owned a little farm not far from Davy's. She was a sensible woman and a good manager. The couple were married in the early summer of 1816. Davy was almost thirty years old. A large group of guests from neighboring frontier farms gathered in Elizabeth's living room. According to one account of the wedding, all the guests were staring in the direction of the doorway through which they expected the bride to appear. Suddenly—to the delight of the children—the unmistakable noise of a grunting pig came from outside the cabin. Then a fat hog strolled into the living room. Frontier farm animals frequently wandered in and out of log cabins.

Davy walked over to the pig and looked at it with mock seriousness. Ushering it out the front door with a wave of his hand, he said, "From now on *I'll* do the grunting around here."

A few months after the wedding, Davy decided to make a trip to Alabama. He was looking for a place with fewer settlers. Game was already getting scarce where he lived. He was eager to move to a wilder region with more wild animals to hunt. He remembered that he had seen some good land in the Alabama Territory, so he decided to look again. Three friends went with him. All of them rode on horseback. After a few days, they reached the area where

Tuscaloosa stands today and decided to set up camp there.

Two hours before dawn, the sound of jingling bells woke the men. Their horses had broken loose and were taking off in the direction of home. Davy volunteered to go after them on foot, carrying his heavy rifle. He pushed ahead for a whole day, wading creeks and climbing mountains, but he couldn't catch up with them. Finally he gave up, figuring that he had walked at least fifty miles.

The next morning he was so sore and tired that he wasn't sure if he could manage to walk any more. But he wanted to get back to his friends, so finally he started on his way. By midday he felt sick and his head began to ache. He was so weak that he had to lie down in the wilderness. Some friendly Creeks came by and offered him a melon, but he was too sick to eat. Using sign language, he asked how far it was to the nearest house. When he learned there was a house only a mile and a half away, he paid one of the Creeks to take him there.

The woman at the house received Davy kindly, putting him to bed right away. Two neighbors heard about Davy's condition and offered to take him back to his companions. He rode first with one and then the other on their horses. By the time Davy reached his friends, he was feeling worse than ever. He couldn't even sit up. His friends arranged to leave him at the home of a man named Jesse Jones so they could continue on their trip.

The Jones family was very kind to Davy. They did everything they could to help him. Later they told

40

him that for five days he had been speechless, and they feared that he would never talk again. But at the end of two weeks he slowly began to improve.

When Davy felt well enough to travel, he asked a passing wagoner to take him to the wagoner's home, which was about twenty miles from Davy's house. On the journey Davy continued to get better. By the time they finally reached the wagoner's farm, he felt well enough to hire a horse to ride home.

Elizabeth was shocked when her husband suddenly appeared at the front door. Davy's traveling companions had returned weeks earlier with his horse. (They had finally found the runaway horses.) The men had told Elizabeth that Davy was dead. They said they had talked to the men who had helped bury him.

Commenting later on the report of his death, Davy said, "I know'd this was a whapper of a lie as soon as I heard it."

Today doctors think that Davy must have been suffering from malaria. He certainly had all the symptoms of the disease. But his terrible experience wasn't enough to keep him from wanting to make another trip. In the fall of 1817 he rode out toward the southwestern part of Tennessee.

About eighty miles from home Davy stopped at a place called Shoal Creek. Here he suffered another attack of malaria. Too weak to travel, he remained there for some time. While he was recovering, he began to like the place so much that he decided to settle his family there.

As soon as Davy was well enough, he moved his family to a plot of land right at the head of Shoal

Creek. He probably realized that the creek would be a good source of water power.

Not long after settling there he used Elizabeth's money, plus loans from friends, to build a gristmill for grinding grain, a powder mill for making gunpowder, and a distillery for making whiskey—all connected—on the stream that ran through his land.

In his autobiography Davy says, "We remained there some two or three years, without any law at all." But Davy didn't have a good memory for dates and events, probably because he kept no records or diaries. Historians learned from studying court records that the county was established on October 21, 1817. In November the state legislature made Davy Crockett a justice of the peace. The first court was held early the next year. Davy knew nothing about legal procedures, and he couldn't write much more than his name. A constable had to fill out official forms. But Davy had the kind of honesty and common sense needed to make a good frontier justice. "My judgments were never appealed from," he later wrote. "I gave my decisions on the principles of common justice and honesty between man and man, and relied on natural-born sense and not on law. . . ." He had never read a law book in his life.

As time went on, Davy improved his handwriting. He began to keep his own records and write them out himself. His wife probably helped him with his handwriting and spelling. She had come from a well-educated family.

One day a Captain Matthews told Davy that he was running for the office of colonel of a regiment. He urged Davy to run for major and invited Davy and his family to attend a cornhusking dance. Davy always enjoyed a good frolic, so he agreed to go. To his surprise, when he arrived at the Matthews farm, a friend told him that the captain's son was running against him for major. Matthews had asked Davy to run for major because he wanted Davy's support in his own campaign to become colonel. He was sure Davy would lose in the race against his son, but he did admit that his son would much rather be running against any other man in the country.

Davy picked an unexpected way of getting even with Matthews. He asked the captain to tell his son not to worry. "Tell him," said Davy, "that I won't run against him for major, but against his daddy for colonel." Captain Matthews had to announce to his large group of guests that Davy Crockett would be running against him for the post of colonel. Another man quickly challenged the captain's son for the position of major. Both Matthews and his son were badly beaten in the election. Davy had become a very popular figure in that part of Tennessee.

Soon Davy was asked to run for state legislature. He agreed without realizing that he would have to "electioneer," as Davy called campaigning for public office. He didn't like the idea of going around making political speeches. Soon afterward he was invited to a big two-day squirrel hunt on Duck River. The hunters were split into two teams. The side that killed the least number of squirrels would have to pay for the barbecue. Naturally Davy's side won. He shot more squirrels than anyone else.

After the barbecue, Davy was asked to make a speech. He tried to get out of it. He knew he couldn't possibly compete as a speaker with the man who was running against him. Finally he decided that he might as well take a chance on what would come out of his mouth. "I got up and told the people I reckoned they know'd what I come for," he later said, "but if not, I could tell them. I had come for their votes, and if they didn't watch mighty close, I'd get them, too." But when Davy tried to say something about the government, the words just wouldn't come out. "And there the people stood," he said, "listening all the while, with their eyes, mouths, and ears all open to catch every word I would speak."

Finally he gave up. He told the people that there had been a little bit of a speech in him a while ago, but now he believed that he just couldn't get it out. They all roared with laughter, so he told a few more jokes that got him big laughs. Then he thanked them for listening, saying his throat was as dry as a powder horn and it was time they wet their whistles a little. When he started off to get a drink, most of the crowd followed after him. Nobody stayed to listen to his rival! The people loved Davy's down-to-earth and warmly humorous approach to campaigning. On election day he got almost twice as many votes as his opponent.

Davy Fights Floods

On September 17, 1821, Davy attended the first meeting of Tennessee's fourteenth General Assembly in Murfreesboro. But he'd barely gotten a chance to get used to his new duties as state legislator when he received word of a disaster back home. The Crockett mills and distillery had been swept away in a huge spring flood. He immediately asked for a leave of absence from the legislature.

When Davy got home, he found a grim sight. Absolutely nothing was left. Three thousand dollars' worth of buildings had been swept away in the churning water. Davy knew there was no way in the world he could get the money to rebuild them. Worse yet, he already owed enormous debts on the property.

After discussing the problem, Davy and Elizabeth decided to sell off all their land and most of their possessions. They had to raise money to pay their creditors. Though Davy didn't mention it in his autobiography, historians believe that Elizabeth and the children must have moved in with relatives for a few months.

Eleven days later Davy returned to the state legislature. He spent most of the first session "learning the ropes." Some of the members were quite snobbish toward him. They came from cities and towns in the eastern part of Tennessee. Many wore suits of fine cloth decorated with a ruffle of white linen. Davy was dressed in the simple frontier clothing that his wife had spun from sheep's wool. One of the members publicly made fun of Davy by addressing him as "that gentleman from the cane." He was referring to the huge tangled canebrakes that grew wild in the western part of Tennessee. The cane was a kind of tall bamboolike grass with thick, hollow stems.

Davy knew that the man was making fun of him, but he refused to be put down. During a break in the meeting, he happened to find a white ruffle lying on the floor. Before he went back to the meeting, he pinned it to his rough wool shirt. When the other members saw the ruffle, they burst out laughing. They understood right away that Davy was poking fun at them and their fancy ways. The member who had made the insulting remark was so embarrassed that he got up and sneaked out of the meeting room.

Davy later claimed that he didn't do much during his first legislative session. The records, however, show that he worked to improve the system of land claims and taxes.

On November 17 the legislature adjourned, and Davy went home. But he didn't stay there long. He had already decided to make another move—farther west. He set out to look for suitable land. His oldest son, John Wesley, and another young man, Abram Henry, went along with him. The three of them hiked about 150 miles—all the way to the Obion River. They were very close to the great Mississippi River, at the far western end of Tennessee. The land was a complete wilderness, but there were Indians hunting in the woods. The soil was rich, and the land covered with giant trees, thick bushes, and tangles of sweet

wild grapes. There was also plenty of wild game—black bear, deer, panthers, possums, and turkeys. This suited Davy just fine.

He picked out a plot of land where he wanted to settle. The nearest neighbors, a family named Owens, lived seven miles away on the other side of the river. The next nearest was fifteen miles away. The three travelers unloaded the supplies they had packed on the back of their one horse. Then they built a rough shelter to keep things safe and dry.

Davy decided to visit his nearest neighbor, but he had no boat to cross the river. The water was so high that it had flooded all the surrounding low country. In the freezing-cold winter, Davy and the two boys had to wade through the river and wetlands. Often John Wesley was forced to swim, and in some places the water was too deep for any of them. Davy would take out his tomahawk and cut down a small tree to use as a kind of bridge over especially deep stretches of water.

When they finally reached dry land, all three of them were soaked and shivering from the cold. To their delight, they soon came to the house where the Owens family lived. Mr. Owens and several men were just walking out the door when Davy arrived. They looked at the water-soaked little group in astonishment. Davy explained who he was and why he was there. Mr. Owens, in turn, introduced the other men. They were boat owners and their helpers, and had come up the river in a boat loaded with flour, sugar, coffee, salt, and other frontier necessities. They were headed for McLemore's Bluff upriver. If they reached the bluff, they were going to get five hundred dollars for being the first to prove that a boat could go all the way up the river. This money would be in addition to the money they would make on their load of supplies.

Mrs. Owens was a kindly, grandmotherly woman. She immediately made hot tea and bundled Davy's small son up in a quilt. Davy and Abram Henry dried themselves by the fire. Everybody stayed at the cabin that night. The boatmen planned to take the boat upriver the next day to a place where a strong windstorm had blown down many trees. The trees had fallen across the river, making boat passage difficult.

In the morning Davy offered to help get the boat through the tangle of trees. However, the men found that the water was too low. Although there was a heavy rain the next day, the water still wasn't high enough. So Davy asked the boatmen to go over to his plot of land and help him put up a cabin while they waited for the river to rise. They agreed. He bought some meal, salt, and whiskey out of their supplies to take with him. In an amazingly short time Davy had his brand-new log cabin.

To repay the boatmen for their help, Davy traveled with them all the way to McLemore's Bluff. At the end of eleven days the men reached the bluff and delivered their load.

In the spring, Davy, the two boys, and one of the men from the McLemore trip cleared a field and planted some corn. Davy also killed ten bears and many deer. During the winter and spring Mr. Owens and his family were about the only other white settlers they saw. But there were still plenty of Indians living there.

Finally Davy decided the time had come to return home. As it turned out, a message had arrived for Davy the day before he and his son came back. Davy had to report at once for a new session of the state legislature. It was now July 1822.

Davy was more active during this second session. He was beginning to understand the business of government. He supported requests to help the poor and needy. He worked to put some order into the system of land claims. Settlers often built cabins, cleared fields, and raised crops on a plot of land only to find that someone else held a prior claim. Sometimes they lost everything they had.

When the legislative session ended, Davy went back to his family and they began preparing for their trip to the new cabin. They began their journey in September. There were now eight children in the Crockett family. In addition to the children each of them had when they married, Davy and Elizabeth now had three of their own.

As soon as the family arrived at their new home, Davy set to work harvesting the corn he had planted in the spring. Then he went into the woods to hunt. He had no trouble supplying his family with meat.

By Christmas, however, he had run out of gunpowder. Without gunpowder, there wouldn't be any meat. A brother-in-law of Davy's had recently moved to the area, settling six miles west of the Crockett cabin. He had brought along an extra keg of powder for Davy, but Davy had never had a chance to pick it up. Now he decided to go after it. Elizabeth protested. The river had flooded again, and the lowlands were covered with water. To get to his brother-in-law's cabin, Davy would have to cross a body of water that was now at least a mile wide. Elizabeth said that they might as well starve as to have Davy drown or freeze to death.

But once Davy made up his mind, he always did what he had said he would do. Bundling himself up warmly and putting on a pair of moccasins, he rolled up a bundle of extra clothes, shoes, and stockings. Then he added a few hunting tools and tied the bundle to his rifle.

The snow was about four inches deep when Davy started out. By the time he reached the water, he later reported, "It looked like an ocean." He waded in and kept going until he reached the channel. He managed to cross by walking on logs floating on the water. Then one of the logs rolled over, throwing Davy into water that was over his head. He had to hold his rifle high to keep it—and his bundle of clothes—from getting soaked.

Finally Davy reached shallow water again. He waded straight ahead until he came to some dry, high land. There he stopped to pull off his wet clothes and put on the dry ones that were in the bundle. By this time he was so cold that his whole body was numb. He decided to run to work up some body heat. At first he could barely walk, let alone run. But after a while it became easier. He somehow managed to cover the five miles to his brother-in-law's house.

Davy arrived late in the evening and stayed overnight. Everyone was amazed to see him. They couldn't believe he had crossed the river. The next morning the weather was freezing cold. His relatives persuaded him not to try to go back home. Instead he went hunting and killed two deer for the family. He stayed two more days, but the weather grew even colder. Davy decided he had to try to get home in spite of the bitter temperature. If he didn't, his family wouldn't have anything to eat. He took his powder keg, his rifle, and his other belongings and started home.

In many places the floodwaters had frozen so hard that Davy could walk on the ice. But there were other spots where the current was too strong to allow the water to freeze. Here Davy again had to wade or walk on logs. Sometimes he was forced to leave the powder keg on a dry spot while he made a trip through the water, carrying his gun. After he had found another dry spot where he could leave the gun, he would go back for the powder keg. He got so cold that he was "nearly frozen to death," but still he kept pushing ahead.

Finally Davy came to a place where the ice was freshly broken. He thought a bear must have done it and was probably nearby. Cold as he was, he primed his gun, ready to shoot the bear if they met. Following the trail of broken ice, he discovered that it led right to his own front door! The trail had been made by the young man from the McLemore trip who now lived with the Crocketts. Elizabeth had sent him out to look for Davy. She feared that her husband was dead.

Davy later wrote, "I wasn't quite dead, but mighty nigh it; but I had my powder, and that was what I went for."

Davy Returns to Politics

On December 25, 1822, the first Christmas the Crocketts spent in their new cabin, Davy and his oldest sons John Wesley and William got up early to fire the Christmas guns. This was a frontier tradition. In fact, it was one reason why Davy had struggled through the ice to get the gunpowder home from his brother-in-law's. When the rifles went off, there was a thundering racket around the cabin. The shots echoed through the frosty early-morning air. Soon answering shots came from neighbors too far away to be seen. This was a common way of saying "Merry Christmas" on the frontier.

The Obion River had frozen solid, and a few days later Davy's brother-in-law came to hunt with Davy and the boys. The brother-in-law was looking for wild turkeys, but Davy wanted to shoot a bear or two. He got his wish. Chasing through the woods, Davy's three dogs began barking excitedly. Davy started after them, but it was difficult walking through the sleet that was coming down. Worse yet, all the bushes were bent and stuck together with ice. When Davy finally caught up, his dogs stood at the base of a tree, barking. He looked up but couldn't see any bear. He was puzzled.

Twice more the dogs did the same thing at two other trees. Again Davy saw nothing. Finally, though, the dogs tracked down the bear. As Davy approached, he saw "about the biggest bear that was ever seen in

55

America." Davy may have been exaggerating—he often did—but it probably was a really big bear. It had climbed to the top of a very tall tree. Davy took aim and fired. The bear came tumbling down. Davy fired two more times to make sure it was dead.

Davy and his brother-in-law, along with the young man who worked for Davy, cut up the bear by the light of a fire. Then they loaded the meat onto their horses and took it back to the cabin. Davy later wrote, "It was sometime in the night before we finished it; and I can assert, on my honor, that I believe he would have weighed six hundred pounds." A six-hundred-pound bear would have been almost twice as large as an average bear.

All during the winter Davy and the boys continued to hunt. There was plenty of venison and bear meat to eat. Davy also collected a big pile of animal furs—bear, muskrat, raccoon, and otter. Now and then he killed a wolf. On the frontier, wolves were seen as a threat to game and livestock, so the state treasury paid three dollars for every wolf scalp a hunter brought in.

In February, Davy loaded his horses with skins and set out for Jackson, a small town about forty miles away. He sold the skins, then bought things he and his family needed—coffee, gunpowder, sugar, and salt. These he packed onto his horses to carry home the next day. Before he left town, he stopped at a tavern to see some old army friends who had fought with him in the Creek war. When a stranger dropped by and found himself in Davy's company, he said he had heard that Davy was a great hunter. "I've even been told," he added, "that you can grin a raccoon right out of a tree."

Davy was face to face with a tall tale about himself. "I'm not so sure about that," Davy answered. "There's an old coon that's been round over yonder for a long time, raiding everybody's cornfield. Whenever we try to catch him, he shinnies up a tree. Then while the dogs are a-barkin' round the tree, he slips over the branches to another tree and leaves 'em there barkin'. If there's anything meaner than an old coon dog barkin' up the wrong tree I don't know what it is.

"Well," Davy continued, "as I was walkin' home one night, I saw a coon in the topmost crotch of an oak tree. I was dead sure it was that rascally old one. The night was moony and clear, and I thought I wouldn't shoot him down. I would just grin him down. So I grinned and grinned, but there he sat with those bright, shiny eyes. I got into a pretty savage humor when he didn't fall, so at last I climbed the oak. But do you know what I found?" Davy looked very serious. "It was nothin' but two big knotholes on a tree that had shed its bark. But those knotholes sure looked just like two eyes to *me*." Davy loved telling stories.

While at the tavern Davy also met three candidates for the new state legislature. One of them, Dr. William Butler, was married to a niece of General Andrew Jackson's. While the men were chatting, somebody suggested that Davy should run for the next legislature. This time he would be a candidate from the district where his new home was located. But Davy said he had no wish to be a candidate. After all, he lived at least forty miles from any settlement. Instead, Davy waved good-bye to his friends and started home.

About a week later a hunter passed by the Crockett cabin. He congratulated Davy for being a candidate for the legislature. Davy didn't know what the man was talking about. The hunter then took a copy of the *Jackson Pioneer* out of his pocket. Pointing to one of the newspaper's columns, he read the announcement of Davy's candidacy. Davy decided that somebody must be playing a joke on him. He told his wife that he was going to get even. He really *would* run for the legislature again! Hiring a man to take his place on the farm, he set out to campaign in the neighboring counties. This time he would run for the office of representative of the frontier counties in the new western district of Tennessee.

As it turned out, four candidates were running for the same seat. At that time the candidates often traveled around the district together, taking turns in making their speeches. Davy usually spoke last.

One day when the candidates stood on a platform together, Davy asked to speak first for a change. The other three men agreed. To their amazement, Davy proceeded to give—word for word—the exact speech that Dr. Butler always made. Davy had heard it so often that he had memorized it. This really flabbergasted Dr. Butler. It left him with nothing to say. When his turn came, he stuttered and stammered, trying to think of something else to tell the crowd.

Although Davy liked to make fun of campaigning, he could also be serious about it. Traveling around his home district in his wool hunting shirt and deerskin leggings, he stopped at every cabin. He would talk to the frontier farmers about their problems and their families. Now and then he gathered a crowd together and made a plain, serious speech. He promised the people that if they elected him to the legislature, he would try to look after them and make sure they got what was due them. Davy was also popular because he often gave the voters a drink out of his flask and a twist of chewing tobacco.

On election day Davy defeated Dr. Butler and the other two candidates. On September 15, 1823, he went back to Murfreesboro as a member of Tennessee's fifteenth General Assembly. This time he knew what to expect and wasted no time getting to work. He was elected to several committees and took an active part in drawing up bills, supporting land claims, and opposing new taxes on poor farmers. He also was bold enough to vote against General Andrew Jackson, the famed hero of the War of 1812 and the Creek Indian wars, when the legislature was selecting a candidate to represent Tennessee in the U.S. Senate.

Davy's term finished on October 22, 1824. Soon after, he decided to run for the United States Congress. That proved to be an election he *didn't* win. His opponent had a lot of experience—and a lot of money to spend on a big campaign. Davy decided to forget politics for a while. He felt it was time to begin improving his financial position. He was now thirty-eight years old and still hadn't acquired the wealth he longed for.

Davy the Bear Hunter

In the fall of 1825, Davy decided to try another business venture. He had heard that there was a good market in New Orleans for barrel staves. Staves are the thin, narrow pieces of wood used to form the sides of barrels and wooden pipes. Since there was a thick white oak forest on the shores of Lake Obion, about twenty-five miles west of Davy's home, he decided to set up his business on the lakeshore. He hired a group of men who were choppers and trimmers to work for him. Some of the men built two big flatboats that would carry the staves down the river. The rest of the workers chopped down trees and split the wood into staves.

Davy worked, too, until he felt that the project was under control. Then he decided it was time to go hunting. He wanted to lay in a supply of meat for the winter. Davy was such a good shot that it didn't take him long to kill enough game to supply his family for the winter. But when he had finished salting down the meat, a neighbor who lived about twenty-five miles away asked Davy to come hunt some bears in his area. He said that the bears were getting very fat and plentiful there. The two men went into the woods for about two weeks and managed to kill fifteen bears. That was more than enough to keep the friend supplied during the winter.

Davy then went back to work with his men at the lake. The boats were beginning to take shape, and already there was a good supply of staves. But Davy quickly got bored. He decided to take one of his younger sons on another hunting trip. They crossed the lake in a small boat and killed three bears the very first evening. The next morning they built a scaffold out of twigged branches. Then they salted the meat and hung it from the scaffold out of the reach of wolves. After that was finished, they went off with their seven dogs to look for more bears. Before long they had killed another three.

While looking for a place to set up camp, they came across a man who was clearing trees and stumps from a plot of land. It was hard work and it paid poorly, but the stranger said he had to earn some money to buy food for his family. They were practically starving. Davy told the man he could help him get more meat than he could ever buy from his earnings.

The next day Davy and his son took the stranger bear hunting. They killed four big fat bears by the end of the day. By the end of the week they had killed seventeen more. Davy gave the man more than a thousand pounds of fine bear meat to take home— enough to last a whole year!

His hunt completed, Davy returned home—but not for long. A neighbor named McDaniel stopped by the Crockett cabin. He said that he was completely out of meat and he wanted Davy to go hunting with him. Davy could never refuse to help a friend. He agreed to go, though he doubted that they would have much luck. He thought that most of the bears would be in their holes, starting to hibernate for the winter.

First Davy and his son took McDaniel to the place

61

where they had killed seventeen bears. They found only one bear there, so Davy decided they should go farther away—to the wild country between Obion and Reelfoot lakes.

Davy, his son, and McDaniel pushed through the rough, brushy country for nearly five miles without spotting any bears. Then they rode past some rocky ridges where they noticed a hole high up in a large black oak. Davy studied the tree bark closely and discovered that a bear had climbed up the tree. But there were no tracks showing that it had come back down. As Davy explained, "A person who is acquainted with bear hunting can tell easy enough when the varmint is in the hollow; for as they go up they don't slip a bit, but as they come down they make long scratches with their nails."

The three hunters got off their horses and set to work. Davy figured they could chop down a small tree and lean it like a ladder against the tall oak. Davy's son could clamber up the slanted tree. Then, reaching the point where branches grew out of the big tree, the boy could climb up the oak and peek into the bear's hole. Davy knew that his son could climb just like a squirrel.

While the men were working, their dogs began to bark. They had found two more bears. Davy and McDaniel went off to shoot those bears, leaving Davy's son to chop down the small tree himself. When they returned, the boy had started chopping down the big tree instead. He had discovered that it was nothing but a hollow shell. McDaniel began to help the boy with his chopping while Davy led the dogs away, down

a hill. He didn't want any of them killed by the tree when it fell.

From a distance Davy looked back and saw the bear's head sticking out of the hole, looking down at his son and McDaniel. Davy hollered to them to look up. When McDaniel saw the bear's head, he grabbed his gun. But the bear was out and scrambling down the tree. McDaniel fired. As soon as the bear touched ground, the dogs surrounded it. They had a rough and tumble fight with the bear as it rolled down the hill toward Davy. Davy lifted his gun and fired, killing the bear.

The next morning Davy left his son at their camp and started off with McDaniel toward a very rough patch of land. A violent windstorm had blown down huge numbers of trees there, creating a dense tangle of trees, bushes, and cane. Here the two hunters killed another bear, cut up the meat, and loaded it onto their horses. Then McDaniel headed back to their camp with the horses.

Davy continued hunting on foot with his dogs. When they started barking in the distance, Davy followed them. Night was coming on, and Davy had a hard time making his way through the rough, hilly woods. As he pushed on, his dogs continued barking. Davy was getting closer to the noise, which meant they had trapped the bear and stopped running.

The woods were now very dark. Davy had a hard time finding the dogs. When he finally reached them, they were at the foot of a tall poplar tree. Davy looked up. In the darkness he could just barely make out a lump in the fork of the tree. There was no moonlight and no dry brush for making a fire to give more light. Davy didn't know what to do. Finally he decided that he would have to shoot "by guess." He aimed at the lump as best he could and fired.

But the bear didn't come down. It just climbed higher, then went out onto a big branch. Now Davy could see it better. He fired again. The bear didn't move, so Davy started to reload. But before he did, the bear was down on the ground among the dogs. A dreadful snarling and scuffling broke out around Davy. He took out his knife, ready to defend himself. But all he could see was one white dog. The other dogs and the bear were so dark that they were completely invisible to Davy. Sometimes the fighting seemed to be less than three feet away.

Suddenly the bear fell into a deep crack that had been made by an earthquake. The big animal seemed to be stuck there. Davy took his rifle and tried to aim the muzzle at the bear's body. Instead, in the darkness, he put the gun against the bear's leg and fired. This only enraged the bear. It jumped right up out of the crack and started to fight with the dogs again. The dogs finally forced it back into the crack. Refusing to give up, Davy grabbed a log that was lying on the ground and punched at the bear with it. When the bear failed to respond, Davy decided that he could safely go down into the crack again. There he thrust his hunting knife into the bear's body, then crawled quickly out of the hole. When the dogs gathered around him again, he knew that the bear must be dead.

In spite of the cold and dark, Davy managed to get the bear out of the crack. He cut up the meat, then stretched out on the ground to get some sleep. But his clothes were wet and partly frozen. He hadn't been able to start a fire to dry himself. He finally decided he had better keep moving or he might freeze. Jumping up and down with all his might, he threw himself around in all sorts of crazy motions. But even this wasn't enough to stop the terrible chills that had seized his body. Then Davy spotted a nearby tree with no branches growing on the lower part of it. Davy shinnied up the tree to the branches, then locked his arms together and slid down to the bottom again. This, he said, made "the insides of his legs and arms feel mighty warm and good." He kept doing this until daylight came—at least a hundred times, he guessed.

The next morning he hung the bear on a branch to keep it safe from wolves. Then he returned to the camp. McDaniel and Davy's son had just about given him up for lost. After breakfast, the three of them went off with their horses to collect the bear's carcass. When McDaniel saw the great crack where Davy had gone after the bear, he said that he wouldn't have gone into it for all the bears in the world. But few men were as persistent as Davy Crockett. As a hunter, he never gave up.

The group hunted a few more days, until they had killed a total of ten bears. This was as much bear meat as they could pack onto their five horses. Davy felt satisfied. During the fall and winter he had killed fifty-eight bears. That spring, he later wrote, "I took a notion to hunt a little more, and in about one month

I killed forty-seven more, which made one hundred and five bears I had killed in less than one year." Historians think that Davy may have exaggerated a little. Probably he was counting all the bears killed by both him and his hunting companions. But one thing is certain. There were few frontiersmen who could match Davy's hunting skills or his determination.

Davy Battles the Mississippi

In January of 1826, Davy turned his attention again to the barrel-stave business. He went back to Lake Obion to see how the men were doing with their work. Both boats were nearly finished, and there were great stacks of wooden staves ready to load onto them. By February the boats were floating on the Obion River, loaded with thirty thousand staves and ready for the trip to the Mississippi River.

But by the time the boats reached the Mississippi, Davy realized that his crews were not really experienced enough to make the journey. None of them had piloted riverboats before, and the boats they had built weren't really fit to make such a trip.

The river current was so strong that Davy decided to tie the two big flatboats together. He figured that this would prevent the boats from becoming separated during the voyage. Unfortunately, by tying the boats together, he made them so heavy and unmanageable that there was no way to guide them properly on the river.

When darkness began to fall, the men tried to land. But they found it impossible to pilot the boats to shore. Other boatmen passing by advised Davy not to try to land. They said he should continue down the river—even in the dark. All night long, though, Davy's men kept trying to land. People at the landing places ran out with lanterns, shouting directions. But there was no way that Davy's crew could follow their advice. They were forced to keep going. Davy wished he was back on solid land hunting bears.

When the two boats were near Memphis, they started floating sideways. Davy was sitting down below in the cabin, warming himself by a fire. Suddenly he heard a lot of noise overhead on the deck. The crew seemed to be running around. Then there was a loud crash and the boat began shaking violently. The trapdoor between the deck and the cabin below broke loose, and water started pouring into the cabin.

The two boats had hit a huge mass of logs and driftwood that had piled up to form a floating island. It was impossible for Davy to get up to the deck. His only hope of escape was through a small hole in the side of the cabin. The men used it to put their arms out when they wanted to dip a pail into the river for water.

Davy hurried over to the hole, aware that it was his last chance. But he could only get his arms and head through the opening. By now the water in the cabin was up to his shoulders. He began to bellow as loud as his lungs could roar.

The crew, who had shifted to the other boat, reached over and began pulling on Davy's arms. He told them to tug till his arms came off, if necessary. It was his only chance of escape. The men pulled as hard as they could. Finally, with a violent jerk, they got him through the hole. In the process Davy lost all his clothes—and some of his skin. But he was so glad to be alive that he didn't complain. Then Davy and his

crew fled from the lead boat onto the floating island—just in time to keep from being pulled down under the driftwood with the boats and all.

The men had to sit on the driftwood all night, even though they were only a mile from land on either side. Some of them had no head covering. Others were barefoot. And one—Davy himself—was totally bare.

As the sun began to rise the next morning, a rescue boat came from Memphis to pick them up. Davy became a big hero—the talk of Memphis. Everyone loved listening to his funny stories and jokes.

Davy made one especially good friend in Memphis—Marcas Winchester. This well-to-do merchant very generously gave hats and clothing to the shipwrecked group. He also loaned Davy some money to tide him over. Davy and another young man took a boat more than three hundred miles down to Natchez, Mississippi, hoping they might see or hear something about the missing boats and staves. Perhaps the boats had broken out from under the drifting island and floated downriver. The two boats and the thirty thousand staves, however, had apparently disappeared forever. Another of Davy's business ventures had ended in disaster. But even though he had lost his boats and all of his barrel staves, Davy was happy just to be alive. He later wrote, "I felt happier and better off than I ever had in my life before, for I had just made such a marvelous escape."

71

Davy Goes to Washington

After Davy returned home from Memphis, he announced that he was going to run again for the United States Congress. The man who had defeated him in the previous election was no longer very popular. Besides, as a member of the House of Representatives, Davy would receive a steady paycheck. After his disaster on the Mississippi, he was sorely in need of money.

Davy's friend Marcas Winchester supported Davy's candidacy. In fact, he lent Davy money for campaigning. Winchester also traveled around the western part of Tennessee, putting in a good word for Davy.

Many town dwellers in eastern Tennessee thought that the notion of sending a bear hunter to Congress was a joke. Newspapers there made fun of this rough frontiersman who wanted to go to Washington. But Davy traveled all over the region, talking to settlers and old army friends. Many were small landowners like Davy. Because he shared their worries and their interests, they believed what he said.

Davy's election district included eighteen counties. It was one of the largest in the nation, in terms of the number of voters. Two other men were running against Davy in the 1827 election. One was Colonel Adam Alexander, who had defeated Davy in the previous election. The other was General William Arnold. Both were wealthy men, well known in Tennessee.

The three candidates often campaigned together. Davy's speeches were always short. He talked plainly about matters that were important to the voters. The other two men made much longer speeches and spent a lot of their time attacking each other. Neither of them paid any attention to Davy. They acted as if they didn't believe a backwoods bear hunter could possibly be elected to Congress.

At one of their joint appearances Davy spoke first, giving his usual short, sensible talk. The other two candidates followed, attacking and responding to each other the way they always did. Neither made any mention of Davy at all. In the middle of General Arnold's speech, a large flock of guinea hens came wandering up to the speakers' platform. They were chattering noisily in a shrill key. The general was so confused that he stopped talking and asked someone to drive the hens away. After he had finally finished his speech, Davy immediately stepped forward.

"Well, General," he said, "you are the first man I ever saw that understood the language of fowls." General Arnold looked puzzled. Davy explained. Because the general had not had the courtesy to mention Davy in his speech, Davy's good friends the guinea hens had come to protest. That was why they were hollering his name: *"Cr-cr-kt-kt! Cr-cr-kt-kt!"* Davy imitated the shrill cry of the hens, shaping the sounds so that they sounded like "Crockett."

"But," Davy added, "you made them stop and drove them all away." The crowd roared with laughter, and the general looked extremely embarrassed.

After all the speeches had been made and the votes cast, Davy Crockett won by a large margin. In November 1827, he left Tennessee. He arrived in Washington by stagecoach in time for the opening of Congress on December 3. Davy had just turned forty-two in August.

In the capital Davy immediately attracted a lot of attention. Although he wasn't wearing his hunter's outfit, he quickly became known as the coonskin congressman.

One congressman from the East decided to have a little fun at Davy's expense. "Mr. Crockett," he said, "I suppose that when you *walked* to Washington you met many alligators. And I suppose you killed them all." Of course Davy had taken the stagecoach, and the congressman knew it. But Davy decided to go along with the joke.

"Well, the alligators *is* pretty thick round my part of the country," Davy answered. "Especially come spring when the lakes are full of water. A short way from our house there's a great deep pool where there's so many alligators that the whole circle's full as a tub of eels. I can sometimes hear 'em roarin' like a horde of bulls. Sometimes they get atop our cabin, and once they knocked the chimney level with the roof and tore off all the bark and shingles. But I don't hunt 'em. I just throw out a rope and snare 'em. Last spring I caught one thirty-seven feet long and tamed him. In summer he comes up beside the cabin and we use him for a bench."

The congressman turned red with embarrassment.

He knew that Davy was poking fun at his snobbish ways. The other congressmen standing around began to roar with laughter at Davy's story. No one like Davy had ever appeared in the congressional chambers. His tall, stocky figure was striking, and he enjoyed using the colorful frontier slang and backwoods humor he had grown up with. He liked to astonish people with his tall tales. His attitude seemed to be: If people want me to be a character, I won't disappoint them.

But Congress disappointed Davy. There were too many dull speeches that said nothing. Too little work got done. "It's harder than splitting gum logs to stay awake," he said. But he was pleasantly surprised to learn that his position gave him the power to appoint people to local government positions such as postmaster.

Some congressmen criticized Davy, saying he had never learned the rules of debate. This wasn't true. Davy's experience in the state legislature had taught him the proper procedures to follow when making a speech.

While Davy was very successful as a colorful celebrity, he wasn't very successful in Congress. He was just too independent and honest to be a politician. He refused to compromise on important issues. One of his first serious undertakings was a Tennessee vacant land bill. He still wanted to get rid of the unfair and unjust treatment of squatters who had been forced off their property by land speculators. This had happened to many of his friends and neighbors. But Congress moved too slowly to suit Davy. As he wrote to one of the people in his district, "There is no chance of hurrying business here like in the legislature of a state." Work on his land bill dragged on and on. As a result, Davy accomplished little of importance during his first term.

In 1828, Andrew Jackson was elected the seventh president of the United States. Jackson was a Democrat with a very different background from previous presidents. He was not a member of a well-to-do, aristocratic family like Washington or Jefferson. Born in a log cabin to a poor family, Jackson was a self-made man who had emerged as a hero from the Creek War and the War of 1812. He was also a successful lawyer, with a large plantation near Nashville and more than one hundred slaves. Davy hoped that Jackson would support the vacant land bill.

Reelected in 1829, Davy returned to Washington for a second term. This time he was full of new hope for his bill. But he soon realized that Jackson no longer supported the interests of the common man. The president seemed more concerned with protecting the rights of wealthy planters and land speculators. They were the ones who had provided the money for Jackson's presidential campaign.

Davy broke away from Jackson. During the summer of 1830, he voted against one of Jackson's pet projects, the Indian Removal Act. This shameful bill set aside $500,000 to move native tribes living in Florida, Georgia, Mississippi, and Alabama off their ancestral lands and into a tract called the Indian Territory. The area later became the state of Oklahoma.

At the end of the Creek War, Jackson had signed a

treaty with the native Americans. Certain lands had been given to them to hold "forever." But soon this territory proved to be very valuable. Gold was discovered in some areas, and in other places the soil was extremely rich, perfect for growing cotton. White settlers began to invade these lands, disregarding all laws and treaties. Armed clashes broke out again between the native tribes and white settlers. A large number of the settlers demanded that the tribes be moved.

Jackson bowed to political pressure and supported the removal. In one of the most tragic episodes of American history, five native American tribes—Creeks, Cherokees, Chocktaws, Chickasaws, and Seminoles—were forcibly removed from their homelands. Greedy white settlers seized their farms and houses and robbed them of most of their possessions.

Davy opposed this forced removal, so he voted against the bill. His vote made public the fact that he was breaking away from Jackson and some of the beliefs of the Democratic party. When he ran for a third term, he lost. His supporters blamed him for Congress's failure to pass the Tennessee vacant land bill. They didn't approve of his voting against President Jackson's bill, either. After all, Jackson was from Tennessee, too. But voters can be fickle. Disappointed by the performance of the man who replaced Davy, they voted Davy back into office in the 1833 election.

Soon the Whig party, a rival of the Democratic party, began to take an interest in Davy. The Whigs disliked Andrew Jackson and his policies. The Whigs were much more cautious and traditional than Jackson's Democratic party. However, they feared that they were getting too great a reputation as a party of rich people. They needed a backwoods personality like Davy Crockett to help their stuffy image. The Whigs began to give parties for Davy, laugh at his jokes, and attend his political rallies. The Young Whigs of Philadelphia even gave him a fancy rifle with his name engraved on a silver plate attached to the barrel. When they finally suggested to Davy that he run for president in 1836, he truly became their man!

To help build his popular image, Davy wrote his autobiography, *A Narrative of the Life of David Crockett of the State of Tennessee.* In it, he presented himself as an uneducated backwoodsman, a remarkable bear hunter, and an honest man intent on improving the laws of his country. Many of the events described in the book are probably true, but Davy had to make himself look as good as possible if he wanted to be nominated for the presidency of his country. So he exaggerated certain things, and a few times claimed to have participated in events that historians know he couldn't have been part of.

For instance, Davy gave eyewitness accounts of two battles with native tribes. Actually, he never saw those battles. He wasn't in the army at the time. He also claimed to have threatened General Jackson with mutiny during the Creek War. While it's true that there was an attempted mutiny, Davy was not in the area when it took place. But more often than not the basic facts in Davy's book are reliable—even if Davy's memory for dates was faulty.

Davy told his story in a straightforward style, letting

his exploits speak for themselves. He used an appealing sort of backwoods language and showed that he had a good sense of humor, even when writing about himself. He undoubtedly wrote the autobiography himself, though he had help with his spelling and grammar. The book was so popular that the Whigs sent him on a grand tour of northeastern cities to promote it and build up a political following. His personal appearances were also successful, but the Whig politicians started becoming disenchanted with Davy. They were no more successful in controlling him than the Democratic party had been. They decided to distance themselves from Davy.

Meanwhile, Congressman Crockett was so busy making speeches that he had little time to attend to his duties in Congress. The people in his district felt that Davy was spending more time representing himself than looking after their political interests. It was a shock to Davy when he lost the next election. He realized that now he would never be selected as a presidential candidate by the Whigs.

Although Davy's political career was finished, he was still a hero all over the country. His autobiography made exciting reading. His adventures fighting Indians, hunting bears, and braving the Mississippi were greatly entertaining to people back East.

Still, Davy's new fame as a kind of legendary backwoods hero couldn't make up for the fact that both the Whigs and his old friends back in Tennessee had abandoned him. Davy decided that the time had come to move on. The frontier had moved farther west, so Davy would go west to catch up with it.

Davy at the Alamo

In October 1835, Davy decided to go to Texas. He was now forty-nine years old and feeling discouraged. He couldn't forget that the voters had failed to return him to office, and now he was back home, no better off financially than when he and Elizabeth made their first move to Shoal Creek eighteen years earlier. Davy felt restless—eager to make a new start— and the newspapers were full of stories about Texas. They said there was plenty of free land in Texas just waiting for men bold enough to claim it.

The province of Texas belonged to Mexico. During the 1820s, after the Mexicans won their freedom from Spain, the new Mexican government encouraged Americans to settle there. It granted large tracts of land to settlers from the States, provided they swore allegiance to Mexican laws. By 1830, such a flood of Americans had arrived that Mexico forbade any more of them to enter Texas. This angered the Americans already there. By 1835 they were beginning to revolt. Davy figured that this kind of political situation might be good for his future. If Texas became a free country, Davy might become one of its "founding fathers."

He and three friends departed by boat from Memphis on November 2. A man standing at the ferry landing when the group set sail later described Davy. "He wore that same veritable coonskin cap and hunting shirt, bearing upon his shoulder his ever faithful rifle." Actually, historians today doubt that Davy wore a coonskin cap during most of his life. But by this time he may have been dressing the way his fans expected the famous frontiersman to dress.

Davy and his friends took a boat down the Mississippi as far as the Arkansas River. Then they traveled up the Arkansas as far as Little Rock. From there they set out overland in a southwesterly direction. Davy wanted to explore the Red River country of southern Arkansas and northern Texas. Their progress was slow. Everywhere they went, people wanted to entertain Davy and his friends. Finally by early January they reached Nacogdoches, in eastern Texas.

By this time the Texas settlers had begun an open revolt against the Mexicans. They wanted to set up an independent country. The situation looked so dangerous that most of Davy's companions decided to go back home. Davy stayed. He felt that he couldn't have come at a better time. If Texas was to have a new government, he might as well be part of it. He swore an oath of allegiance to the provisional government of Texas or any future republican government that might later be declared.

The Texans gave a great banquet in his honor, and Davy made a speech. "I was for some time a member of Congress," he said. "In my last canvass, I told the people in my district that if they saw fit to reelect me, I would serve them as faithfully as I had done; but if not, they might go to hell and I would go to Texas. I was beaten, gentlemen, and here I am." The crowd applauded him wildly. Davy was campaigning again!

He moved on to San Augustine, Texas, not far from the Louisiana border. From there he wrote his last letter to his oldest daughter, Margaret. In it he told her, "The cannon was fired here on my arrival and I must say as to what I have seen of Texas it is the garden spot of the world. The best land I ever saw . . . and I do believe it is a fortune to any man to come here. . . . I have taken the oath of government and I have enrolled my name as a volunteer and will set out for the Rio Grande [River] in a few days with the volunteers from the United States. . . . I am in hopes of making a fortune yet for myself and family. . . ."

Davy joined a group of fifteen volunteers headed for San Antonio de Béxar, in southern Texas. There was a fort in Béxar called the Alamo. Built by the Spanish as a church and mission, the Alamo had been turned into a fortified garrison—a large, sprawling group of buildings that covered four acres (an area about the size of a city block). In the center was a rough rectangle of bare ground called the plaza. Around it stood several buildings, including a long two-story barracks. Most of the buildings were connected by stone walls. The old church itself was in ruins—part of the roof was gone. Nevertheless, it was still the strongest building in the fort. Its walls were four feet thick.

The Alamo was separated from the town by the winding San Antonio River. The fort's only source of water was a ditch that ran from the river to the fort. A small group of about 112 men were stationed there under the command of Colonel James C. Neill. On January 18, General Sam Houston, in charge of the Texas military forces, sent Colonel Jim Bowie with thirty men to the Alamo with a message. He urged

Colonel Neill to blow up the fort and retreat north with his men to join Houston's army.

Jim Bowie was one of Houston's most trusted officers. Already a legend on the frontier, he had roped and ridden alligators, and along with ten friends he had once fought off 164 Indians for two days. Tall and sandy-haired, he had proved himself a born leader. He had also won fame for his skilled use of a special long knife that became known as the Bowie knife.

Bowie seldom followed orders if he thought they were wrong. Looking around the Alamo, he decided that it would be a mistake to abandon the fort. Instead of ordering a retreat, he began to organize the men, working out a plan to strengthen the fortifications and repair some of the damaged places. Colonel Neill wasn't eager to stay at the Alamo, but he couldn't stand up to Bowie's growing enthusiasm.

About nine days after Bowie's arrival, a scout rode into Béxar. He said he had seen about two thousand troops under the command of General Antonio López de Santa Anna gathering near the Rio Grande on the border between Texas and Mexico. A few days later another scout brought word of five thousand more Mexican soldiers heading north. No one at the fort took the news very seriously. The numbers seemed exaggerated. Besides, they thought, the troops would certainly take several months to reach the Alamo.

On February 3, Colonel William Barret Travis appeared at the Alamo with thirty men. Travis was a career soldier, eager to make a name for himself. He very much wanted to see Texas break away from Mexico. Travis had studied law before joining the army. He was more formal and proper than Jim Bowie.

At first the two men clashed. Both were touchy and easily offended. Travis thought he should be in charge because he was a regular army officer. Bowie thought Travis, at twenty-six, was too young to be commanding him. Finally they decided to share the command. During this struggle for power, Colonel Neill gradually faded into the background. He finally decided to go on sick leave. He left the fort and never returned.

On February 8, five days after Travis's appearance, Davy Crockett rode into the Alamo with fifteen companions. Though only three came from Tennessee, the group was soon nicknamed "The Tennessee Mounted Volunteers." Crockett's fame had preceded him. Everyone—the soldiers at the fort and the citizens of Béxar—stopped what they were doing and rushed to the main plaza to greet the great man. Someone quickly got a packing case, and Davy climbed onto it. After telling some of his best stories, he explained how he happened to be in Texas. Then, turning serious, he said, "I have come to your country, though not, I hope, through any selfish motive whatever. I have come to aid you all that I can in your noble cause. I shall identify myself with your interest, and all the honor that I desire is that of defending as a high private, in common with my fellow citizens, the liberties of our common country."

With Davy's arrival there was now a force of about 142 men at the Alamo. Though few in number, the men were experienced and tough. None of them really wanted to retreat. Still, they would need reinforcements. On February 18, Travis sent a messenger, James Bonham, to Fort Defiance in Goliad, a town about ninety-five miles from Béxar. There was a force of at least 420 troops at Goliad under the command of Colonel James Fannin. Travis begged Fannin to send help.

Two days after Bonham left for Goliad, another scout returned to the Alamo and reported that Santa Anna's forces were crossing the Rio Grande. For some reason the men at the Alamo still didn't really believe this. They should have. By this time the advance guard of Santa Anna's forces was only 119 miles away.

On the morning of February 23, the men at the fort noticed some unusual activity in the town of Béxar. Many of the Mexican families were packing up and leaving. They had been warned that Santa Anna's forces would soon be entering the town. Travis became suspicious and sent Dr. John Sutherland and another man out on horseback to scout the nearby countryside. He also sent a second messenger to Fannin at Fort Defiance, pleading for immediate help.

Suddenly everyone began working furiously. Some of the men herded the cattle into the fort. Others carried in big sacks of grain and other food supplies. Women and children who were related to soldiers in the fort left their houses in the town to seek refuge in the Alamo. In the middle of all this excitement, Travis heard a clattering outside the gates. Dr. Sutherland and his companion had returned from their scouting expedition. They reported that they had spotted

Santa Anna's troops, with their gleaming armor, from the top of the nearest hill.

Davy Crockett had been the first to greet the doctor. "Colonel," Davy said to Travis after hearing the doctor's report, "what can I and my fifteen boys do? Assign me a position and we will try to defend it."

Travis had just the place for them. There was a palisade, a kind of fence made of stakes and earth, running from the church to the barracks. It was a weak link in the defense. But with Davy and his sharpshooters to guard it, the fortification wouldn't be weak any longer. The rifles of the Tennessee Volunteers were accurate at a range of six hundred feet. The Mexican smoothbore rifles could barely hit a target just two hundred feet away.

Later in the day, Dr. Sutherland and his companion started off on another mission to recruit reinforcements. This time they headed north to the town of Gonzales. As the two men rode off in one direction, Bonham was returning from another. He was bringing bad news to his friends at the Alamo. Colonel Fannin had refused to send reinforcements.

By this time Santa Anna and his advance troops were marching into Béxar and spreading throughout the town. From their positions in the fort, the Texans watched some Mexican soldiers hang a red flag from the church steeple. They knew what the red flag meant. No surrender. No mercy.

That evening Jim Bowie collapsed. For the past few days he had been getting sicker and sicker. Not even the doctor could figure out what was wrong with him.

Now Bowie had no choice but to give up and go to bed. He turned over all responsibility to Travis.

The next day, February 24, the Mexicans began firing some of their cannons. The Texans crouched at their posts, dodging flying dirt and stones. Davy and his Tennessee boys kneeled behind their palisade, taking shots at the enemy whenever they got a chance. In the dark little rooms alongside the church, the women and children huddled. As night fell and the cannons stopped, Travis surveyed the damage. By some miracle, not one Texan had been killed or even hurt.

The next morning the Mexicans started firing again, moving forward and taking cover behind the houses and shacks. One group even crossed the river and began to install heavy weaponry in some of the huts and shacks near the fort. At last the big Alamo guns began to blast—from the church roof, from the stockade, and from the main entrance. Davy's men joined the fight with their rifles. Davy himself was everywhere, cheering the men on. Some volunteers rushed over to lend their support. Everyone seemed to want to fight beside Davy.

Near the fort, a group of Mexicans set some old huts on fire. A group of soldiers rushed out of the Alamo gate to put out the fires. Davy and his men stood on the palisade protecting them with their long-range rifles. The Mexicans watched helplessly. Their smoothbore rifles couldn't touch Davy and his men.

When the fighting finally died down, Travis once again checked his troops. Amazingly, there still were no casualties. Two or three men had been hit by flying rocks—nothing worse. But over in Béxar more Mexican reinforcements had arrived. The Mexican artillery batteries were moving forward and digging in. Travis decided to send a messenger to the commander-in-chief, General Houston, to ask for help. He didn't know that Houston was away from his home base for several days. In his message Travis praised the bravery of his men, especially the Honorable David Crockett, who had continually tried to rally the spirits of the troops.

Davy's Last Stand

The next few days were relatively quiet at the Alamo. The Texans saved their ammunition as much as possible and spent their time making sure everything was ready for the next battle. The riflemen, however, stayed at their posts, firing at any Mexicans who tried to cross the river. One Mexican captain later wrote:

> A tall man with flowing hair was seen firing from the same place on the parapet during the entire siege. He wore a buckskin suit and a cap all of a pattern entirely different from those worn by his comrades. This man would kneel or lie down behind the low parapet, rest his long gun, and fire, and we all learned to keep at a good distance when he was seen to make ready to shoot. He rarely missed his mark, and after he fired he always rose to his feet and calmly reloaded his gun, seemingly indifferent to the shots fired at him by our men. . . . This man I later learned was known as "Kwockey."

"Kwockey" had to be Crockett.

During the next few days the Alamo defenders could see that more and more Mexican troops were moving into place, gradually surrounding the fort. The Texans continued to hold fast. They were now convinced that they must hold out until the rest of

89

Texas woke up. Word came on February 28 that Fannin was on his way with troops. But that hope proved short-lived. Fannin had indeed started, then changed his mind. Three of his wagons had broken down and all of his oxen had wandered away, so Fannin decided to strengthen the fortifications at Goliad instead of going to the Alamo.

Then on March 1 a small miracle happened. Thirty-two men arrived from Gonzales at three A.M. They had managed to sneak between two enemy artillery units. The weary men defending the Alamo were delighted to see some new reinforcements—even if there were only thirty-two of them. The following day—March 2—Texas declared its independence from Mexico, but the men at the Alamo knew nothing about it.

By March 5, Santa Anna had really tightened his noose around the fort. There were Mexican gun batteries only six hundred feet from the walls. Travis called his men together and told them they had three choices: to surrender, escape, or fight to the end. Only one man, Louis Rose, chose to leave. Both Davy and Jim Bowie—who had been brought out on a stretcher to encourage the men—tried to talk Rose into staying. He refused, and managed to sneak safely out of the fort. Meanwhile, Travis continued to send out messages pleading for help.

At five A.M. on March 6, Santa Anna finally struck with full force. Ever since midnight, eighteen hundred of his best men had been silently getting into position under the cover of darkness. At the first sign of dawn they attacked, shouting, "Viva, Santa Anna!"

The lookout on the wall raced toward the barracks,

yelling, "Colonel Travis, the Mexicans are coming!" The Texans scattered in all directions as they scrambled to their posts. The Mexican troops had already reached the ditch around the fort. They were raising planks and ladders against the wall. Travis stood at the north battery, aiming his shotgun down at the invaders. Suddenly a volley rang out. Travis spun around. He had been hit in the head. He fell down into the fort, stunned and dying.

All around, the Texas artillery and rifles blazed away. The whole fort was brightly lit by the blazing guns. Davy's so-called "weak" palisade proved to be very strong. He and his sharpshooters turned back waves of Mexican attackers. The Texans were battling with a wild fury. But in the end there was no way 170 men could withstand the combined force of eighteen hundred Mexican soldiers. Santa Anna's troops battered at the wooden gates and stone walls of the stockade, trying to break in. Twice they were driven back by heavy gunfire. On the walls the defenders— Davy among them—shot cavalry leaders and infantrymen rolling the cannons forward. But the Mexicans simply pushed over the dead bodies of their comrades, advancing closer and closer to the walls of the fort. Finally they managed to climb over the north wall and pour into the sprawling Alamo compound.

At the end, the brave men of the Alamo were defending themselves by fierce hand-to-hand combat. But their knives, tomahawks, and rifle butts were no match for the sharp Mexican swords and bayonets. The enemy battered down the heavy doors of the old church itself and overwhelmed the last defenders.

For many years people insisted that Davy Crockett had died during the final battle, using his rifle as a club after his ammunition was used up. Since all the Texas soldiers were killed, no one was left to give the Texas side of the story. A later account, written by an officer on Santa Anna's staff, told a different story. Colonel José Enrique de la Peña said that seven men had been taken alive. "Among them," he reported, "was one of great stature, well proportioned, with regular features, in whose face there was the imprint of adversity. He was . . . David Crockett, well known in North America for his unusual adventures. . . ." According to de la Peña, some of the Mexican officers urged Santa Anna to spare the seven prisoners, but he ordered that the men—including Davy—be killed by sword immediately. Today many historians believe that this account may be the most reliable.

Whatever the precise facts, Davy died on March 6, 1836. He was almost fifty years old.

Santa Anna's attack on the Alamo enraged the whole country. News of the terrible massacre spread fast—even though there were no telephones or telegraph lines. Newspapers all over the country reported the tragedy, and people everywhere sent money and men to support the Texans. It took less than two months for the Texans to get their revenge. Shouting "Remember the Alamo!" the forces of General Sam Houston destroyed Santa Anna's army on April 21 in the battle of San Jacinto. The independence of Texas became a fact. The dream of the men of the Alamo was realized.

The 170 brave defenders who died at the fort had

come from almost every state in the union. They were farmers, craftsmen, professional men, and adventurers. All had loyal friends and loving families back home who mourned their loss. But no one's death was mourned more widely than Davy Crockett's. He had gotten to know people all over the country. They had come to think of him as a friend—and a hero. In death he had displayed the same determined and courageous spirit that had moved him all of his life. The *Natchez* (Mississippi) *Courier* seemed to speak for many Americans when it wrote shortly after his death:

Poor Davy Crockett!—We lament the fate of the sick Bowie—we feel sad and angry, by turns, when we think of the butchery of the gallant Travis—but there is something in the untimely end of the poor Tennessean that almost wrings a tear from us. It is too bad—by all that is good, it is too bad. The quaint, the laughter-moving, but the fearless upright Crockett, to be butchered by such a wretch as Santa Anna—it is not to be borne!

Yet if Davy Crockett died at the Alamo, his death also brought him a kind of rebirth. He was reborn not as a man but as a legend. After his death, the many stories, fanciful tales, and recollections about him grew and spread. The combination of all the stories, full of imagination and bigger than life, have come to be the legend of Davy Crockett. But how does a legend come to be? And how does a legend differ from the real person it is about?

94

The Legend of
Davy Crockett

Davy himself may have begun the legend of Davy Crockett when he published his autobiography. In it he described his amazing rise from an unknown backwoodsman to a national figure. The book sold so well that publishers quickly put together two other books to appear under the Crockett name. They hired other authors to write the books, but Davy probably received some money for the use of his name.

The same year that Davy headed for Texas, a new kind of Crockett book was published. It was called *Davy Crockett's Almanack of Wild Sports of the West and Life in the Backwoods.* The book drew a little material from his autobiography, and it included some stories that Davy was supposed to have written himself. The almanac was so popular that a whole series of Davy Crockett almanacs appeared over the next twenty-five years. They combined frontier tall tales with information on the weather, the stars, and medical treatments. In them, Davy's adventures sounded like the exploits of a folk superhero.

Nearly all of these almanacs were published after Davy's death, and everything in them was larger than life, depicted with broad strokes of imagination. According to one story, the infant Davy Crockett had been rocked by water power in a twelve-foot cradle made from the shell of a six-hundred-pound snapping turtle. Even as a child, the almanacs stated, Davy could walk like an ox, run like a fox, swim like an eel, yell like an Indian, and rumble like an earthquake. Storytellers had Davy walking underwater on the bottom of the Mississippi River and kicking the sun loose from its frozen axis. His knife Big Butcher became the longest in all Kentuck, and his dog Teazer was credited with overpowering a buffalo. Davy was said to roam the West with his pipe-smoking pet bear Death Hug and his singing buffalo Mississip.

During the summer following Davy's death, a book about the Alamo was published. It was called *Col. Crockett's Exploits and Adventures in Texas . . . Written by Himself*. To explain how Davy could have written the book even though he died at the Alamo, the publisher claimed that a Texas soldier had found Davy's notes in the pocket of a Mexican officer. Supposedly the enemy officer had removed the notebook from Davy's pocket. Actually the first few chapters of the book were based loosely on letters Davy had written after he reached Texas. But a man named Richard Penn Smith is believed to be the real author of most of the book. Whatever the book's origins, most readers were convinced that it was truly Davy's journal, written in the Alamo. The book was a best seller. Everyone wanted to read about the brave defenders of the fort.

The almanacs continued to keep the Alamo legends alive right along with the Davy Crockett legends. One of the stories claimed that "Colonel Crockett's body was found . . . with his big dagger in his hand, and around him were lying seventeen dead Mexicans, eleven of whom had come to their deaths by his dagger, and the others by his rifle and four pistols, which lay beside him. . . . He had received two musket balls in his body. . . ."

Another almanac contained an even more amazing account: "It was calculated that during the siege he killed no less than eighty-five men and wounded 120 besides, as he was one of the best rifle shooters of the west, and he had four rifles, with two men to load constantly, and he fired as fast as they could load, nearly always hitting his man. . . ."

Without a doubt Davy was courageous and a master sharpshooter. He surely must have put his great skills to work at the Alamo. But stories of his performance there were often exaggerated. Most of the writers were from the East and had no real knowledge of frontier life. The stories were pure fiction, and the fantasy became more and more exaggerated as time went on. Before long, Davy became a national legend. People everywhere discussed his bravery, his tall tales, his clever sayings, and his daring and courageous exploits. There were even people who claimed that Davy hadn't died at all. The Crockett almanacs printed a steady stream of reports about people who claimed they had seen Davy—sometimes as a slave laborer in a Mexican mine, other times trapping grizzlies high in the Rocky Mountains. For many years people continued to keep the legendary Davy Crockett alive.

In the 1950s the Disney Studios gave Davy a whole new life in a popular television series. Suddenly an incredible Crockett craze swept the country again. Stores were filled with raccoon tails, coonskin hats, toy Crockett guns, powder horns, and moccasins. And the legendary Davy came to life again on the big screen in the person of the famous movie actor John Wayne. The film, made in 1960, was called *The Alamo*.

The real Davy Crockett would certainly have enjoyed his enormous popularity. All his life he had looked for fame and fortune. He didn't live long enough to make his fortune in Texas, but he did become world famous for his bravery at the Alamo. Nothing would have pleased Davy more than the fame he earned in Texas—except, perhaps, the fact that he is still remembered today, more than 150 years after his last brave stand.

Highlights in the Life of
DAVY CROCKETT

1786   Davy Crockett is born on August 17 in what is now eastern Tennessee.

1796   John Crockett, Davy's father, opens a tavern in Jefferson County, Tennessee.

Tennessee becomes the sixteenth state of the Union.

1798   John Crockett hires Davy out to Jacob Siler.

1799   Davy starts school but runs away from home to escape a punishment.

1802   Davy returns home after an absence of two and a half years.

1803   Davy works for two farmers, paying off his father's debts.

1806   Davy marries Mary "Polly" Finley on August 16.

1811   Davy, Polly, and their two sons — John Wesley and William — move to Lincoln County, Tennessee.

1812   On June 1, the United States Congress declares war on Great Britain.

On August 30, Creek warriors attack Fort Mimms, Alabama.

1813   Davy moves his family to Bean's Creek in Franklin County. He calls his homestead "Kentuck."

99

In September, Davy joins the volunteer militia for a ninety-day enlistment. Under General Andrew Jackson, he takes part in the massacre of Creek Indians at Tallussahatchee on November 3.

Davy returns home on December 24.

1814   In March, General Jackson defeats the Creeks in the battle of Horseshoe Bend.

On September 28, Davy reenlists and helps look for British-trained Creeks hiding out in the Florida swamps.

On December 24, the Americans and British sign the Treaty of Ghent, ending the War of 1812.

1815   In March, Davy returns home from Florida.

In May, Davy is elected a lieutenant in the 32nd Regiment of the Tennessee militia.

In the summer, Polly Crockett dies.

1816   During the summer, Davy marries Elizabeth Patton, a widow with two children. He sets off to explore Alabama, almost dying from malaria on the way there.

1817   The Crockett family moves to Shoal Creek in Lawrence County, Tennessee.

In November, Davy becomes a justice of the peace.

1818   Davy is elected colonel of the 57th Militia Regiment in Lawrence County.

1821   Davy's mills and distillery are destroyed in a flood.

Davy wins a seat in the state legislature and attends the first session on September 17.

In November, Davy explores the Obion River region with his oldest son, John Wesley.

1822   In July, Davy attends the second legislative session. In September, after the end of the second session, the Crockett family moves to western Tennessee, near the Obion River.

1823   Davy is reelected to the state legislature. He attends the first session on September 15.

1824   Davy's second legislative term ends in October.

1825   In August, Davy loses the election for U.S. Congress. He decides to set up a new business venture, making barrel staves.

1826   In February, Davy nearly drowns when his boats loaded with barrel staves are wrecked on the Mississippi River.

1827   Davy wins a seat in the U.S. House of Representatives.

1828   In December, Davy arrives in Washington, D.C., for his first session in the U.S. Congress.

Andrew Jackson is elected seventh president of the United States.

1829 Davy is reelected to Congress.

1830 Davy opposes the Indian Removal Act.

1831 Davy loses his election for a third term in Congress.

1833 Davy is elected to a third term in Congress. The Whigs court him as a potential presidential nominee.

Davy publishes his autobiography, *A Narrative of the Life of David Crockett of the State of Tennessee,* and begins a tour of the northeast, promoting his book.

Davy loses his bid for reelection. The Whig party deserts him.

1836 Davy signs an oath of allegiance to the provisional government of Texas.

In February, he arrives at San Antonio de Béxar.

On March 2, Texans declare their independence from Mexico. Four days later, on March 6, Davy Crockett and the last of the Alamo defenders die in their beleaguered fort.

On April 21, General Sam Houston's troops destroy Santa Anna's Mexican army at San Jacinto.

For Further Study

More Books to Read

Davy Crockett. Naunerle Farr (Pendulum Press)

Davy Crockett. Felicity Trotman (Raintree Steck-Vaughn)

Davy Crockett: An American Hero. Tom Townsend
  (Eakin Press)

Davy Crockett at the Alamo. Justine Korman
  (Disney Press)

Davy Crockett: Defender of the Alamo. William R. Sanford
  (Enslow Publishers)

Davy Crockett: Frontier Adventurer. Dan Zadra
  (Creative Education)

Davy Crockett, Young Rifleman. Aileen Wells Parks
  (Bobbs-Merrill)

Quit Pulling My Leg! A Story of Davy Crockett.
  Robert M. Quackenbush (Prentice-Hall)

Videos

The Alamo: Thirteen Days of Glory. (Fries Home Video)

Davy Crockett. (Agency for Instructional Technology)

Index